MILLIONAIRE
HOUSEWIVES

MILLIONAI₹E HOUSEWIVES

From Homemakers to Wealth Creators

Rinku Paul | Puja Singhal

Foreword by Anu Aga, ex-chairperson, Thermax Ltd

PENGUIN
EBURY
PRESS

An imprint of Penguin Random House

EBURY PRESS

USA | Canada | UK | Ireland | Australia
New Zealand | India | South Africa | China

Ebury Press is part of the Penguin Random House group of companies
whose addresses can be found at global.penguinrandomhouse.com

Published by Penguin Random House India Pvt. Ltd
7th Floor, Infinity Tower C, DLF Cyber City,
Gurgaon 122 002, Haryana, India

First published in Ebury Press by Penguin Random House India 2017

Copyright © Rinku Paul and Puja Singhal 2017

ISBN 9780143429296

Typeset in Adobe Garamond Pro by Manipal Digital Systems, Manipal
Printed at Thomson Press India Ltd, New Delhi

www.penguin.co.in

To my dad,
Miss you more than words can ever say
Rinku

~

To my family,
You are the wind beneath my wings
Puja

Contents

Foreword

This book on women who have braved so many odds to find their calling, and are now doing what brings them joy, makes for fascinating reading. Many of them decided to be entrepreneurs because of financial reasons or unfortunate personal circumstances. Their stories of determination and hard work, their intermittent failures and their eventual triumph over all odds show us the rich potential in taken-for-granted homemakers. The women entrepreneurs featured in this compilation are true heroines, who never allowed themselves to give up but fought back with a vengeance to improve their lot.

All their stories have a common refrain—of embracing change, taking chances and staying focused even in the face of repeated adversity. They learnt to live with the inevitable guilt that comes from having to balance the demands of home and their workspace.

Reading the experiences of these remarkable women took me back to a phase in my own life when, as a trained social worker inexperienced in the ways of running a company, I had to join Thermax, first to assist my ailing husband and then, following his sudden demise, to run it. Like some women featured here, I too grieved in solitude for the immense loss I had faced, but then I picked myself up to do what had to be done. I learnt the importance of asking for help and was not afraid to admit my ignorance.

Women still tend to live by the old rules set down by society. In varying degrees, internalized beliefs about themselves and their roles limit them, whether they are employed or are entrepreneurs in their own right. In a globalized economy, it is imperative that we create a nurturing environment that can help women write their own scripts, not just for economic reasons but to build a just and empowered India.

This book offers women insights to gain courage and confidence to take the plunge and embark on their own entrepreneurial adventures. I think the accounts of these twelve successful housewives-turned-entrepreneurs will help answer some pertinent questions that women face, as they try to break out of the cocoons of their routine lives or when they have to start afresh, unsure of the choices they need to make.

There is a story, a lesson, an anecdote, an inspiration for everyone in this book. I hope it pushes more women out of their comfort zones and fires them up to strike out on their own. As Canadian mayor and feminist Charlotte Whitton said, 'Whatever women must do, they must do twice as well as men to be thought half as good. Luckily, this is not difficult.'

I wish the book and its authors, Rinku and Puja, the publishers and readers the very best.

Anu Aga
Former chairperson of Thermax Ltd; Padma Shri recipient

one of they could arrange and threaten him to come out
on this point. As Canadian troops and Canadian battalion
Whereas this Canadian ... cannot quite do that, and the
more would all go on to be thought half as great Canada
the first was allowed.

... the doctrine of the regiments maintained. This, the
... doubt in the academic observer here.

... ...
France thought war to Hamilton Ltd. It is a base complaint.

Introduction

In 2016, taking a cue from our own career arcs, we chronicled the stories of women who dared to give up well-paying corporate careers to follow their passion in our first book, *Dare to Be*. The response was overwhelming. So many women reached out to us to say that the stories had given them hope as they stood on career crossroads themselves. It showed us that meaningful storytelling can be a great change agent.

It was with this thought that we approached the stories of homemakers who had turned to entrepreneurship. Come to think of it, the homemaker has little or no say in society, primarily driven by her lack of financial independence. If at all she finds a mention, the portrayal is stereotypical, often exaggerated; she is depicted either as a Desperate Housewife or as the all-sacrificing mother.

The fact remains that the changing dynamics of society and the desire to retain one's individuality are slowly leading the homemaker to reinvent herself beyond her call of duty as a wife or mother alone. This is not an easy transition for few have people to hold their hand through the ups and downs of this journey. While we may have heard the iconic Lijjat-Papad tale of an enterprise which began with a seed capital of Rs 80 and has today grown to become a large women's cooperative employing over 45,000 women, or encountered some 'mompreneurs', overall there is no robust storytelling around the many challenges that homemakers-turned-entrepreneurs face.

First and foremost, the transition from the role of a homemaker to that of an entrepreneur requires tremendous grit in overcoming one's own mental blocks, which result from a lack of experience and/or qualifications. Not only does the woman have to reskill herself for the new role, her family also has to reboot itself for change. Add to this the fact that there is the perpetual voice of naysayers willing to write her off even before she has begun, and, of course, that finding funding is a huge challenge, and you can see why these stories are worth telling. There is the added concern for the woman for she has to balance both her work and home life. In fact, in the course of the several conversations that morphed into this book, one of the women reminded us that the term 'homemaker-turned-entrepreneur' is in itself a misnomer, as even after she becomes an entrepreneur, the home still largely remains the woman's responsibility. Her growing to-do list, as depicted on the book cover, stands testimony to her multifarious roles.

The women featured in the book are diverse, both in the circumstances that propelled them towards entrepreneurship and in the challenges they had to face in their journey. While some of them were pushed towards entrepreneurship on account of unfortunate events striking their hitherto secure worlds, others had strong financial compulsions that made them turn to entrepreneurship and yet others had a niggling sense of wanting to do something beyond their traditional roles. From being first-generation entrepreneurs to taking on the challenge of running a business legacy despite their inexperience, there is a range of stories in this book. The stories are also varied in the fact that these women took to myriad industries—from those thought to be more woman-oriented to those which were considered absolute male bastions. What makes these stories even more powerful is that they are told in the voices of the women.

Although their motivations, their struggles as well as the sizes of their businesses are different, there are some common lessons that emerged from each of their lives that can come in handy for others who want to undertake this incredible journey too. Here are only a few of them:

✓ **It is only when you start thinking of the enormity of the problem that you start getting pulled down by it:** To say that these women had to face numerous difficulties is to state the obvious. Yet, they consciously did not let anything—be it their lack of experience or the absence of relevant qualifications—come in their way. If anything, they went on to substitute these with their commitment and passion, which helped them tide over every difficulty.

✓ **Homemakers are intrinsically good managers:** While these women started out their entrepreneurial journeys by taking baby steps, in hindsight, they realized that homemakers already know all the principles of running an enterprise—from controlling inventory to making purchases, from producing goods to providing consistent quality, from satisfying customers to delivering on time, they do it all. All that they need is a little more faith in their own abilities.

✓ **It is important for women to spend time, money and effort on their own development:** Each of these women has said that the need to reskill oneself for the new role is crucial. In fact, the biggest stumbling block the homemaker-entrepreneur faces is that she often relegates herself to the bottom of her priority list, and feels guilty when she spends time and money on developing her own skills. It is time to rejig that equation and, armed with the right skills, get ready to take on the world.

✓ **The case of the elusive work-life balance:** All of these women talked about the working mother's guilt in particular and the importance of a strong support system to tide one over the initial uncertain period. The good news, however, is that they discovered that growing up with a working mom is often the best training that a child can get—in time management, independence and much more. The key to work-life balance, they feel, also lies in not expecting perfection from oneself.

✓ **There is no right time to start:** Many of these women have demonstrated that it is never too late to give wings to one's dreams. If you are passionate about something, it doesn't matter how old you are; the important thing is that you need to get started. It is imperative that you do not lose nerve in the initial period when the going is tough. While every business goes through a gestation period, the entrepreneur needs to have faith in her vision, and has to put in the time and effort to make it successful. In fact, it is only if one is passionate about their work that they can survive the many difficulties that are bound to come in the way of a new venture. Without passion, one is likely to get buried at the first hit.

✓ **Beyond a point, one needs to follow one's own trajectory without bothering about what people say:** As women entrepreneurs, most of our interviewees have met naysayers who have constantly told them that they are not likely to succeed. The need for societal approval is, in fact, one of the primary reasons why so many women end up giving up on their dreams. However, it is the ability to ignore sceptics and critics, and keep oneself motivated, that distinguishes a successful woman entrepreneur from others. The key clearly lies in being attuned to one's own inner voice instead of that of naysayers.

When read in isolation, many of the above lessons may seem clichéd. However, distilled from real-life experiences, they are proof that anyone can build their own destiny. In fact, the only reason that these women have bared their hearts and souls, sharing not just their professional but also their personal journeys, is so that other women can be inspired to live their own dreams.

We'd like to make two important clarifications here. The first: this book isn't intended to be a compilation of business case studies. While we documented the journeys of homemakers who became millionaires, we learnt that earning money wasn't their sole driving force. In referring to them as millionaires, we are alluding to their financial status, yes, but we are also referring to their will power, which is worth a million dollars and which has propelled them to their current positions. In that sense, this book is an ode to the human spirit that, despite overwhelming odds, can achieve what it sets out to. If this book can inspire other women setting out on this life-changing journey, it will have achieved its purpose.

The second: while the book celebrates entrepreneurial journeys, our aim is not to detract from the tremendous contribution made by those women who have stood by their choice of being homemakers. Their roles are no less demanding as they run their homes like clockwork and traverse the complex terrain of modern-day parenting. There is also no denying the sheer gumption of stay-at-home moms who have put their careers on hold to be with their children during their formative years. In fact, many of the homemakers-turned-entrepreneurs that we spoke to also identified with their roles as mothers before anything else and gained huge satisfaction from raising children who contribute to society and stand up for the community.

1

Ambika Pillai

~

Acclaimed hairstylist and make-up artist; founder, Ambika Pillai Brand of Salons with a turnover of over Rs 10 crore

Moment of Truth: Walking out of a loveless marriage of seven years, with a small child in tow.

Ambika decided to become a homemaker at the age of seventeen, hoping that marriage would give her a break from her studies, which she struggled with for she was dyslexic. By the time she was twenty-four years old, she had a broken marriage behind her and the Herculean task of bringing up her child alone. All of this, with no educational support to fall back on. Four decades later, not only is Ambika Pillai a household name with her chain of salons but she is also extremely sought after when it comes to Bollywood as well as high-profile fashion events. Her achievements include a number of awards, primary among them being The *Femina* Power List 2015, Kerala Business Woman of the Year 2014 and the *Vogue* Best Make-up Artist 2011.

The Long-Promised Road

'The only thing that overcomes hard luck is hard work.'
—Harry Golden, writer, socialist

Clichéd as it may sound, I was born with the proverbial silver spoon in my mouth. My father was a successful cashew exporter and my childhood, spent in a sprawling mansion in the backwaters of Kerala, was nothing short of idyllic. As the second of four girls, I shared a very close bond with my parents and sisters. My early memories include travelling to the most exotic places in the world with them.

By the time I turned five, my sisters and I were sent to boarding school in Ooty and that is when trouble started brewing in my otherwise perfect world. That no one knew of dyslexia in those days meant that I was considered a dumb kid throughout my growing up years. If I took a verbal test, I would probably score 100 per cent, but when it came to reading or writing, I was a total disaster. Have you ever heard of anyone repeating classes two and three? I did. By the time I got to class seven, my parents realized that something was amiss and thought I would do better under their wings. I was then brought home to Kollam. That, of course, did little to improve things on the academic front. Seeing me struggle up to class ten, my father asked me if I wanted to study further or if I wanted to get married. No marks for guessing what I chose. Going to college wasn't an option at all in my head; I saw marriage as my ticket to freedom.

At the tender age of seventeen, my life took a decisive turn when a prospective groom came to see me. I didn't even know his name. The one thing about him that impressed me though was his impeccable English. He had an MBA degree, was a gold medallist no less, and I gave up my world without any reservations to follow him to his. The excitement didn't last long though. Despite his seemingly bright prospects, the reality check arrived as soon as I moved in with him to a tiny single-room apartment in Calcutta, a far cry from my sprawling home in Kerala. I was expected to wear a saree, be up at 5 a.m., cook, clean—things that I had never done before. I didn't protest, refusing to let any of this affect me since I wanted to make my marriage work. I began to take many other things in my stride; being made to feel that I was not good enough on account of my lack of education was only one of them. I would have lived with all of this, but ours really wasn't a marriage at all.

Not once in five years did we have a physical relationship. It was hard to explain this to my parents, who were convinced that my inability to bear a child meant there was something medically wrong with me. Trips to doctors, medical tests and even surgeries were my lot as I found it very hard to tell my parents the real issue with my marriage. I had to literally beg my husband to have a child and, thankfully, my daughter, Kavitha, was born after five years of marriage. If I had thought that a child would improve matters, I was living in a fool's paradise as things started going from bad to worse.

Finally, with a two-year-old child in tow, I mustered up the courage to walk out of my seven-year-old marriage. I went back to my parents' place. In retrospect, those seven years were one of the scariest times of my life. Kids should not get married as young as I did; at that age, you don't even know your own mind, forget the other person's. From wanting to be a happy housewife to coming back to my parental home in the throes of depression, I had come a long way. I had spent the last seven years of my life in a loveless relationship and had absolutely nothing to fall back on. If there was one thing I was grateful for, it was Kavitha. In fact, till this day, if anyone asks me if I regret my marriage, my answer is a vehement no, only on account of my daughter.

I just had no idea what I would do next. In my seven years of marriage, I hadn't acquired any skills that could stand me in good stead. While my parents were supportive, my dad's suggestion of letting him 'look after' my child and me financially didn't go down well with me. With my other sisters married by then, I remember asking my father if I could help him with his cashew business—wanting to become the son he had never had. His answer, however, was a resounding 'no' as he felt it wasn't a woman's job. He couldn't picture his daughter socializing with his many customers—a part and parcel of his cashew export business.

Never in my life had I felt like such a total loser. I wanted to stand on my own feet, but in the absence of any skills, I saw all doors closing in on me. In my desperation, I even came up with naive options like selling T-shirts on the beaches of Goa, where my lack of education would not be a deterrent. It was on one such day, when I was feeling totally dejected, that I saw an advertisement by Shahnaz Hussain in the local newspaper, inviting students for a hairstyling course in New Delhi. I made up my mind to join it. More than anything else, my decision was based on the fact that being a beautician didn't require me to be a graduate. My father, of course, was devastated by the idea of me stepping out of the home turf. My mom tried to buy peace by explaining to my dad that at least I was choosing a 'woman-oriented' career and that I would be back home after finishing my course.

I landed in Delhi, a totally unknown city, with my daughter in my arms, utterly terrified of what the future held. I had never lived all by myself before or taken any independent decisions. Yet, here I was, fending for myself, looking for accommodations to rent. The problem was further compounded by the fact that I didn't speak any Hindi. Irrespective of the many problems staring me in my face, I knew that there was no turning back now. I had to do this—more for my daughter than anyone else. While Delhi now feels like home, in those days I was a rank outsider. I remember people calling me '*kali kaluti* (dark complexioned)'. Of course, the saving grace was that since I didn't know the language, I couldn't quite understand what it meant. I somehow held on, and managed to finish two beauty courses.

Upon finishing my courses, although my parents were keen that I return home, I took up a job at a small two-seater parlour, which paid me Rs 2000 per month. I paid Rs 1000 as house rent and tried to stretch the balance to take care of my child. Money was something I never had to worry about in the past and these were trying times to say the least. While my father had paid for my courses, I was now determined to seek minimal financial help from him. I remember trying to save money from the measly Rs 1000 I had left after paying rent in order to buy a moped bike that would make commuting easier. Today, if one of my staff members tells me that they want to leave because they have a better offer, I never hold them back for I have witnessed the struggle for money first-hand.

The one bright spot of my life throughout this period remained my daughter, who was three years old by then and had just about started school. I remember telling Kavi stories of my own childhood—how I visited Disneyland when I was thirteen years old and how I would ensure that she did the same, although I had no clue how I would fulfil this promise.

Despite knowing that I had the support of my family and that if nothing worked I could always go back to them, it was not an option for me. Life, I must admit, wasn't easy. In one of my early jobs, a customer walked into the salon and I was designated to attend to her. Having been with me at the same boarding school, she soon recognized me as Gopinathan Pillai's daughter and was absolutely taken aback to see me there. In her indignation, she even walked up to the salon's owner to tell her that the father of the girl she had employed at such a puny salary could buy out several salons like hers. The owner obviously didn't take this dressing down well, to the extent that I was fired from that job on some pretext in no time. Heartbroken and worried about my finances, I turned to a hair stylist, who had been my teacher in one of the courses. She helped me find a new job. One day, the owner of the salon, impressed by my English-speaking abilities, asked me to man the billing counter. I was quite taken aback to see that a salon made as much as Rs 30,000 in a single day. This was 1990–91 and Rs 30,000 meant a lot of money then.

This is when I spoke to the hair stylist who had got me the job and I suggested that we strike out on our own. She agreed on the condition that while the salon be named after her, I would have to put in all the money. Keen to set the project rolling, I agreed and reached out to my dad to borrow Rs 7 lakh from him. By then my dad had realized that I wasn't coming home in a hurry. Imagining his daughter working for a small salary, driving a moped and trying to fend for herself in an alien city were images that didn't sit well with him, so he willingly agreed to fund my venture.

The next seven years went by in a flurry of activity as the salon that we set up became quite popular. My personal life though continued to remain tumultuous. I was heartbroken when my ex-husband (my divorce had come through around the time Kavi was three) decided to send Kavi to Bangalore to study, stating that I was not capable of providing her with a stable life.

It was somewhere during this time that I met Rakesh, aka Rocky, at a party, and he totally swept me off my feet. He pursued me like nobody had ever done—sending me flowers, taking me to the fanciest of places. I, however, wanted to be absolutely sure that the person I now married would give my daughter and me the stability we deserved. It was after four years of relentless pursuit that I gave in and agreed to marry him in the hope that my life would now change. However, the fun and laughter he brought into my life wasn't meant to last. He was heavily into drinking and gambling. There were nights that he would never come home. It was as if the four years we had spent together were a complete lie. There was zero stability. It was over in no time.

If I thought that this time around I at least had a career to fall back on, even that was not to be. I learnt from a trusted source that money was being pilfered from the business that we had so painstakingly set up. I had given so much of myself to the business that I was absolutely heartbroken. However, on starting to notice the discrepancies myself after this tip-off, I decided to call off the partnership. The fact that I wasn't even returned my initial investment made things really tough for me. Kavi was back with me by then and this was a time when I didn't even have enough money to buy bananas for her. My first entrepreneurial outing had backfired and how!

One day, when I was walking down a street, I happened to bump into Harmeet Bajaj, a fashion choreographer who knew me from my salon days. She asked me if I was available to style some models' hair for a show. It didn't take me a second to reply in the affirmative. Surprised, she asked me if I needed to consult my diary for the dates, not knowing the tough financial situation I was in. Anyway, I went on to do the show, for which my work was very well appreciated. There was no looking back from there.

The next big show I remember doing was with fashion designer Hemant Trivedi, for which I flew down to

Mumbai. After styling the hair of the models, he asked me if I could do their make-up too. I had no idea how to do make-up at the time, but gutsy as I was, I said yes. I asked for some advance payment to buy a make-up kit, telling them that I was not carrying mine (when, in reality, I didn't possess one). Having asked the models which make-up shades were doing the rounds then, I ran down to pick up the necessary stuff from a local shop. Needless to say that when it was time for Hemant to see the first model whose make-up I had done, I was awfully scared. To my luck, Hemant found my work brilliant and I was on the road to success. One thing led to another, and I landed the role of doing Aishwarya Rai's make-up for the movie *Taal*. I remember Karan Kapoor (Shashi Kapoor's son) calling me up and ensuring that I was sitting down before he broke the news to me—I had won my first IIFA (International Indian Film Academy) Award for Make-up. Till today, this award remains special for me.

Somewhere along the way, I set up my own salon—this time in the rented accommodation I lived in, with a friend as partner. Unlike the last time—where I had put in all the money and a whole lot of effort, but I was only a shadow of my partner—this time around, it was a source of immense pride for me to name the salon 'Visions by Ambika'.

During the initial period though, the going was far from easy. I remember how I had to sell my jewellery to pay my staff their salaries for six months. However, at the end of six months, the salon started doing brisk business. From doing the make-up for one bride in six months to doing dozens of brides a day, we were suddenly the talk of the town. People had to call for appointments; the waiting period was as long as three months.

However, I still hadn't learnt my lesson. It was around the time Kavi wanted to go to Parsons School of Design in New York to study, when, for the first time, I asked to see the books of accounts. I realized that they were in a complete mess. So much so, that although I recalled doing the make-up for twenty-two brides out of the 180 that walked into the salon on my birthday, the books showed that only two brides had come in that day. I had clearly been cheated yet again.

Devastated does not even begin to describe how I felt that day, especially because I believed I had let Kavi down. Eventually, she had to apply for a student loan when all my life I had worked only to secure her future. The drama that unfolded when I confronted my partner was something else. I was threatened, got pushed out from my flagship salon and literally had to start all over again, this time with loans hanging over my head.

Nonetheless, I stood up once again, and worked day and night to set out on the path to recovery. With my determination and god's will, I have twelve salons today, with a total staff strength of over 200. This, after having started out with a single salon that had a staff strength of six. Today, I also have salons in Kochi and Thiruvananthapuram, and I am close to my roots again.

I take great pride in the fact that my daughter is now fully involved in the business; in fact, I am looking forward to taking the back seat now. My passion currently lies in making my own herbal products as I find the process therapeutic. I have often taken many of these herbal scrubs and face packs I make to the Fashion Weeks and have given them to the models. If I could have my way, I eventually want to turn the entire salon into a chemical-free zone. Actually, I have already taken the first step in this direction. My herbal range of products called 'Kaytra by Ambika Pillai' is slated to hit the market soon.

If you ask me what my biggest learning as an entrepreneur has been, it is that one cannot just sit back and look at the creative aspect of business alone without worrying about the financial aspect. I believe that handling money doesn't come very easily to creative people sometimes and we are happy handing over this responsibility to someone else. Fact is, we need to be far more astute financially—this is the only way we can safeguard our own interests.

Given my life journey, I am often called to give speeches at women's forums. Really, the only piece of advice I have for everyone is to stand up for themselves, irrespective of their situations in life. Your destiny clearly is in your own hands. I have had homemakers ask me how they can overcome their myriad fears and do something for themselves. To them, I always say that my story is proof that you can shape your own destiny. Life, I believe, is all about taking chances. I took mine. Walking down the tried and tested path just because everyone else is doing it isn't a good enough reason. You need to explore and do what you feel passionate about. Having said this, it is a fact that the entrepreneurial journey is riddled with difficulties—more so when you do not have any prior experience with running a business. But you have to start somewhere. It is your own inner strength that will stand you in good stead and take you far. Even if someone tells you that they are there to support you, know that it is you who has to support yourself.

Of course, I have derived my strength from my family—Kavi, my mum, my sisters. I knew that no matter what happens, they will always come running to help me, just the way I would do anything for them. My dad was a very important part of my life. The day I lost him, I thought my life had ended. In a way, every success I have been able to achieve was to prove to him that as a woman I could still make him proud. When I was leaving home, he was worried that I would bring a bad name to the family. At that time, I wanted to tell him that he was discounting me only because I am a girl. Had it been his son, he would have blessed him to go out and make a life for himself. I wished he had trusted me a little more at that point. I think his words have remained with me and I was conscious that I should not do anything that would have people talking badly about me, thus hurting him in the process.

My career has seen many high points—my numerous awards, the fact that I have worked for Bollywood and for royal families, and have been the only hairdresser from India to be invited to the L'Oréal hairdressing convention in Paris, among others. However, my greatest achievement remains that I was able to fulfil the promise I made to my daughter to take her to Disneyland when she was thirteen years old. I gave her the childhood I was privileged to receive. The first time I bought a Mercedes car, I looked up to the heavens and hoped my dad was watching me, as that is the car he drove. Irrespective of my material success, however, if I look back, I think every single day that I have spent with my daughter is a huge blessing for me. Even those days when I had landed in a new city and was running my home with just Rs 1000 a month were special in their own way as they were filled with my love for my daughter and the hope of giving her a great future.

Life Lessons

✓ One cannot just sit back and look at the creative aspect of businesses alone. It is important to deal with the financial aspect as well.

✓ Always stand up for yourself, no matter what.

✓ Your destiny is in your own hands.

✓ No matter how many people claim to support you, it is you who has to stand up for yourself.

✓ Life, I believe, is all about taking chances.

✓ You cannot only walk down the tried and tested path. You need to do what you are passionate about.

✓ The entrepreneurial journey is riddled with pitfalls, especially if you do not have any prior experience in running a business. But you have to start somewhere.

✓ Your inner strength can see you through the arduous journey.

✓ My story is proof that you can make your own life.

2

Savita Chhabra

~

Vice chairperson and director, Hygienic Research Institute Private Limited, manufacturers of Streax Hair Colour and Super Vasmol 33 Kesh Kala, with a turnover of Rs 400 crore

Moment of Truth: The untimely death of her husband that led her to step into his shoes, though she hadn't so much as operated even a bank account earlier.

For twenty years, Savita Chhabra's world centred on her home and hearth, comprising her husband and two sons. Until fate dealt a cruel hand—a cardiac arrest claimed her husband's life suddenly. Within five days of his passing away, this homemaker had to step into her husband's shoes. A period of intense struggle and immense learning followed, but she (along with her sons who joined the business after completing their education) has been instrumental in making Hygienic Research Institute a Rs 400-crore company. Being awarded the National Award (2007) and the Outstanding Woman Entrepreneur of the Year Award (2007) are only some of the feathers in her cap.

An Eventful Journey

'Life can only be understood backwards; but it must be
lived forwards.'
—Søren Kierkegaard, Danish philosopher

Perhaps the only dream I harboured as a young girl growing
up in Chandigarh was to get married. This dream came true
at the tender age of nineteen when I fell in love with a distant
relative. My parents weren't too happy about it, considering
that I was still in my second year of college. For my father,
who had made his way up in a government job, education
was not something that could be compromised. My would-
be-husband solved this dilemma when he promised that
marriage would not put an end to my education. True to
his word, I went on to complete my studies post wedding.
In fact, I appeared for my final-year examinations when my
son was about a year old. It was not an easy feat, but I had to
honour the commitment made to my father. My education

(or its lack) wasn't the only issue that my parents raised at the time of the wedding. They were also apprehensive about the fact that my would-be husband's leg was afflicted by polio and that he had a slight limp. They wanted to make sure that a decision taken in the naivety of youth should not weigh me down in the later years. However, head over heels in love, I was totally convinced about my choice—a decision that worked out in my favour for the next two decades.

I went on to build a happy home; and with two sons born in quick succession, our lives were nothing short of blissful. Amidst my familial duties, I also kept myself gainfully occupied with learning several new skills. The years saw me learn painting, cooking, typing and even enrolling in a Montessori course. My husband was a second-generation entrepreneur who ran a hair-care products manufacturing company along with his brother. Set up by my husband's father in 1957, Hygienic Research Institute (HRI) was one of the oldest companies dealing with cosmetic products in India. Having started off small, the company now had a turnover of around Rs 2–3 crore and our lives were happily chugging along. Not that I had much information about the company's operations. Even if I tried asking my husband about simple stuff, like how the company worked, he would laugh it off saying I did not need to bother myself with such mundane stuff. Such was the nature of the times, when it was believed that women needed to be protected from the vagaries of the world.

Life, however, has no guarantees, as I was soon to realize. On a cold day in December, after having spent twenty blissful years together, life changed forever. We had had a Christmas party at home the previous night and when my husband felt a little uneasy at work the next morning, he put it down to fatigue and decided to head back home. Only he had a cardiac arrest on the way and even though he was rushed to the hospital by his driver, he didn't survive. When I received the news that he was in hospital, I was putting together his clothes for another party that we were scheduled to attend that evening as part of the year-end celebrations.

To say that I was devastated would be an understatement. That life could be so ephemeral came as a huge jolt to me. But I didn't even have the time to grieve for myself. Overnight, I suddenly had to play the role of both mom and dad to my two sons, who were fourteen and nineteen years old at the time. My elder son was pursuing his second year of pharmacy in Pune, while the younger one was in class ten. Both of them were at an impressionable age and I had to ensure they were not totally shattered.

The circumstances demanded that I forget my own loss as a wife and stand up as a strong mother for my sons. My husband's death was a huge blow for the business as well. While my brother-in-law looked after the sales function, my husband took care of the operational aspect of the business and clearly that end could not be left loose.

Needless to say, my family was extremely worried about me and it was a unanimous call made by my family and my in-laws that my elder son drop his studies to step into his father's shoes. This is something I could just not allow. My son was brilliant at his studies and I did not see any merit in jeopardizing his future. Besides I did not want to let him live with the regret of not having completed his studies for no fault of his own. I made up my mind that I would be the one to take over the reins of the business.

This decision didn't find any supporters, as everybody felt that I had neither the experience nor the technical qualifications to pull this through. Besides, I had led a very comfortable life, and people felt that I didn't have a fighting chance when it came to the male-dominated world of manufacturing. No obstacle, however big, could deter me in the face of the fact that if I didn't take this step, I would be jeopardizing my son's future. Against everyone's counsel, I stepped into office just after my husband's fourth-day ceremonies were over. With his passing away, there was the need to execute a fresh partnership deed and clearly this issue could not be left in abeyance for long.

In a jiffy, my comfortable life disappeared. Not only was there a huge emotional vacuum that needed to be filled but there was the fear of stepping into absolutely unknown territory. I was also worried as my younger son would be all by himself at home, preparing for his class ten exams at that time. My husband used to help him with his studies.

In fact, the last sentence my husband said to me as he left for work that fateful morning, was to tell Ashish that they would begin with his biology syllabus from that evening. I made it a point to use the time I spent commuting to work to make notes for Ashish, which I could discuss with him when I got back home in the evening.

I had joined HRI at a time when the set-up was fairly small—the operations only had fifteen–twenty people in all. The senior management, used to a certain style of functioning, wasn't too happy with a woman at the helm. I can never forget this one factory manager who was particularly unhappy with the prospect of reporting to me and who left no stone unturned to make my life difficult. While I was very keen to get a hang of the business, this manager only gave me some petty jobs to do. I remember spending countless hours in the office with tear-filled eyes, wondering how I would learn when I was kept away from anything remotely important. There is one piece of advice that a dear friend gave me that I will never forget. She said that even if I sat at home, I would cry about the tough hand life had dealt me. It was best, therefore, that I cry in office and make something of my life. I decided to do just that.

The turning point came when this manager had to go on leave on account of a family exigency. In his absence, I gathered the courage to file a mandatory excise challan that needed to be filed by the fifth of every month. Having successfully worked on the figures, I remember how I spent a lot of time worrying about a 3-paisa difference that was appearing in the accounts. In my naivety, I didn't know that such a small difference could easily be rounded off. I still recall the manager entering the office on the day of the filing, and how shivers ran down my spine as I thought of what he would have to say when he saw the papers. I stood rapt in attention while he went through each and every paper, and finally pronounced the judgement—I was ready to run the company by myself now.

As a woman and a newbie to the company, there were enough instances where I undermined my own capabilities and people, of course, continued to be sceptical of my talents. In the early days, a driver once flung aside the vehicle keys, telling me that he did not want to work for me when I asked him a lot of questions in a bid to improve my understanding of the logistics chain. He perhaps felt that I doubted his integrity. While such instances did impact me at the time, in the long run, they only went on to fuel my resolve of never giving up in my new role.

Experience, of course, is the greatest teacher and over the years I learnt the nuances of the business. After completing his studies over the next two years, my elder son joined the business. Together, we took a number of decisions that helped the company move from strength to strength. Primary among them was changing the packaging of our flagship product, Vasmol, and introducing new variants of it. Doing this was a bit of a risk as especially in the rural areas, the product was recognized by its packing—the '*neela dabba* (blue packaging)'. However, I felt that we had to upgrade the product to keep up with the times. The move worked well for the company. Later, we went on to launch another product that changed the dynamics for us—Streax Hair Colour.

I recall how we hired a US-based technology firm to help us develop the product. Once it was ready, I asked some beauticians to try out the product and, unfortunately, they did not give it great feedback. We were ready to send the product out into the market, but this immediately became a big red flag for us. We had to put the project on hold and rework its formulation. It was a big decision at the time, albeit the right one, and today, Streax has gone on to become the market leader in terms of volume of sales. For me, each incident like this has only proved that one cannot rest on past laurels and that quality cannot be compromised.

Later, of course, my younger son also joined the business. Today, all of us have different portfolios but a common vision for the company.

Being a woman, I did face a lot of trust issues in the beginning, but I think that being a woman entrepreneur comes with its own set of advantages. I believe the strong emotional connect I have been able to build with my teams can be put down to my being a woman and the empathy that comes with it. While it has been twenty-six years now since I took my first faltering steps into HRI, there are three teachings of the Vedanta that have stood me in good stead—the three Cs of Commitment, Competency and Consistency; and I am still working on each one of them as I move along.

In my experience, most restrictions on women are self-imposed. We end up second-guessing our own abilities, perhaps because of the several lessons that are ingrained in us from an early age. The fact, however, is that there is nothing that women cannot achieve. Just the other day, I was at a forum speaking to homemakers and I was telling them that homemakers are naturally gifted. All the principles of running an enterprise are already known to them—be it inventory control, ensuring consistent quality or timely deliveries, they do it all. I recall how one of the women in the audience stood up to say that despite all this, the work that housewives do is least appreciated . . . Till you stop doing it, I had added on a lighter note.

For homemakers who are aspiring to be entrepreneurs, all you need is a lot of confidence to know that you can handle any situation. You also need to learn to manage the working woman's guilt. It is true that you need to devote time to your children, especially in their early childhood. The important thing, however, is to manage your time and balance your roles as much as possible. Sometimes, in our zeal to do our best for our children, we end up overprotecting them. In fact, growing up with a working mother is the best training you can give your children—both from the perspective of time management and value for money. Both my sons have settled well in the business today and are happily married. Nothing gives me greater joy than to think that I managed to fulfil all my roles to the best of my abilities.

Today, other than my active involvement in the business, I like to spend time giving back to society. I have recently joined hands with a non-governmental organization called Global Foundation, and we are providing skill development and training to young people. It was a pleasure to see five out of the twenty-five kids who were trained to become electricians in one of our skill development projects, starting their own businesses and providing employment to several others. I have also recently set up a corrugation plant and a major share of its earnings will go towards social welfare. There is nothing quite as rewarding as seeing lives being transformed.

I am often asked what have been the proudest moments in my long and eventful journey. There are several; receiving the National Award for Business Excellence is certainly one of them. As I went up to receive the award from Manmohan Singh, then the prime minister of India, my whole life's journey flashed before my eyes. The other extremely proud moment for me was when my granddaughter wrote about how I am her role model in her university application essays. I was not just happy to know that my granddaughter thought so highly of me, but the fact that she had a woman role model gave me great satisfaction. Women often internalize all the subtle messages society sends them about their place in the world, and it makes me glad to know that for my granddaughter, and hopefully for other young women, an alternate worldview is emerging. One where women are equal partners.

Life Lessons

- ✓ When I look back, I realize how fear held me captive, even when it came to simple tasks.
- ✓ A lot of restrictions on women are self-imposed. We constantly second-guess our own abilities.
- ✓ The natural empathy I feel as a woman has helped me develop an emotional bond with my teams.
- ✓ Homemakers already practise all the principles that help in the efficient management of an enterprise—be it controlling the inventory or delivering on time.
- ✓ All we need is a whole lot of confidence to know that we can handle any situation. And we also need to overcome the working woman's guilt.
- ✓ Growing up with a working mother is the best gift we can give our children.
- ✓ If you are looking to start something of your own after a long break, the first thing you need to do is upgrade

your skills. Believe in the fact that once you set out, solutions will appear.

✓ Commitment, competency and consistency: these three Cs have held me in good stead.

✓ It makes me happy to know that my granddaughter has internalized the message that women are equal partners.

3

Nita Mehta

~

Celebrated author, publisher, restaurateur and entrepreneur, with a turnover of over Rs 8 crore

Moment of Truth: An unsuccessful attempt to bake a birthday cake for her husband and the ridicule that followed triggered in her the resolve to learn everything about baking and eventually share her craft with the world.

Starting up at a time when women's participation in the workforce was negligible and start-ups were considered far from glamorous, Nita Mehta went on to build a successful business empire based on her passion to whip up a great meal. The homemaker who started off running cooking classes from her home has put India on the global culinary map today. She wears many hats—renowned cooking instructor, best-selling author, restaurateur and is now trying her hand at retailing food products. At the age of sixty-five, there is no stopping this powerhouse of energy and talent.

Follow Your Heart

'Let yourself be silently drawn by the strange pull of
what you really love. It will not lead you astray.'

—Rumi, poet, scholar

Growing up as a woman in small-town Bhopal in the
1960s rarely meant setting your eyes on a career. It was
a given that once I graduated from college, I had to get
married and 'settle down' into domesticity. My passion
for food boded well for a would-be homemaker. In fact,
when I look back, I see that I inherited my love for food
from my mom. An unassuming lady, she had the knack
of whipping up a delicious meal in a jiffy. As a child, I
remember how even the ubiquitous dal in our house tasted
heavenly and was relished by my friends as if it were a
delicacy. To my mom's credit, she went out of her way to
encourage my love for cooking. I would often volunteer
to make tea when we had visitors at home and my mom

patiently obliged, while keeping a watchful eye over her young child of course. What really drew me to the kitchen though was the aroma of freshly baked cookies. Seeing my love for the culinary arts, my parents encouraged me to pursue home science at Lady Irwin College. I must admit that those years at college taught me not just the basics of cooking but also organization and discipline, which are critical to the art and science of cooking.

Once I graduated, it was time to settle down into holy matrimony, except my parents couldn't find a suitable boy just then. With time on my side, I went on to pursue my post-graduation in food and nutrition. A year down the line, my parents found an extremely broadminded groom. He had recently returned from the USA with a master's degree in IT—this wasn't as commonplace then as it is now. He was extremely keen that his fiancée be well educated and encouraged me to finish my post-graduation. I must admit that at that stage, as a young girl on the threshold of a new life, another year of studies did seem a bit tedious to me. Today, however, I cannot thank my husband enough as that course gave me an essential understanding of the nutritive value of various foods and this knowledge has stood me in good stead.

My marriage was put on hold for a year till I finished my post-graduation, and I graduated with a gold medal, no less. After this, I entered a huge joint family as a coy bride. With no career ambitions per se, I quickly settled down into my new life. A large family meant more opportunities to cook and many more people to savour my cooking, and that kept me contented. The one adjustment that I did need to make was that unlike me, my husband's family was totally vegetarian, which meant that I had to polish my vegetarian cooking skills.

One incident from those early days still stands out in my memory. Close on the heels of my wedding was my husband's birthday, a rather important occasion for a young wife. I decided to make the day special by whipping up a homemade cake. Only that, for the life of me, I didn't quite know how to bake an eggless cake. I turned to my sister-in-law for help. However, she decided not to part with the full recipe and left out some ingredients. This resulted in a rather hard cake, which wouldn't even let a knife pass through.

As a bride of just twenty-two, all the fun my family made of me, despite being in jest, left me teary-eyed. I promised myself that day that I would not just learn, but master the art of baking eggless cakes. It was this resolve that led me to bake cakes that soon became a hot favourite not just with my family but also with the neighbours and the many visitors who frequented our house. One of the people, who absolutely relished my cakes, suggested that I start taking classes to teach other women this art. With time to spare, I decided to take up the suggestion seriously.

In those days, a working daughter-in-law was a rarity and my in-laws weren't too happy with the idea of me taking up cooking commercially. My husband, however, was very supportive and wanted me to work on my passion. The fact that I would not be stepping out of home was some sort of consolation for my family and they reluctantly agreed to the idea that I take classes. I remember placing a small advertisement in the newspapers for my baking classes and being flooded with calls.

While cooking may have been my forte, this was my first brush with managing business affairs, and I learnt scheduling and time management among other things when I started running these classes. To my delight, I had women from all walks of life attending the classes I ran from a single room in my house. The high point came when the supplement of *Hindustan Times*, *HT City*, praised my classes, stating that I detailed the recipes so well that people were able to exactly recreate the cakes. This article saw many more women signing up for my classes. The fact that we had a good time in the classes, creating and then tasting our delicacies, added to their popularity.

The one thing I always ensured was that amidst all this, I did not abandon my duties as a daughter-in-law. I believe that homemakers are often held back by the fear that stepping into an entrepreneurial role may mean that they will end up neglecting their families. This isn't necessarily true. With some amount of time management, it is indeed possible to run both your home and enterprise successfully. At least, my experience says so.

It was while conducting these classes that the idea of writing a cookery book came to me. My husband was already writing some computer books at the time and had access to publishers. We reached out to some of them to see if they would be interested in a cookbook, and most of them seemed positive about the idea. I was hugely encouraged by this and set out to write the book immediately. What I didn't realize was that I had little experience and no training in the many aspects that writing a cookbook involved. The content, of course, was my strong suit. I spent long hours, often up to 1 a.m., in the kitchen, trying out each recipe to ensure that people could exactly replicate the dish in their homes.

However, ensuring that the content was complemented with attractive pictures was a different ball game altogether. I hired a professional photographer and would cook the dishes much before the pre-decided time of the shoot, only to see that the dishes in the pictures didn't look appetizing at all. It was only later, through much research and trial and error, that I learnt that food needs to be only half-done for the photo shoot and that it shouldn't be kept too long after cooking.

I remember how I had to pay through my nose once again to redo the entire shoot. However, nothing could stop me from moving ahead in the journey that I had set out on. Unfortunately, all these efforts came to naught when I went back to those very publishers who had assured me that the subject would be of interest to them; they refused to publish the book. I cannot begin to describe how disheartened I was. However, I was certain that my efforts would not be wasted and I told my husband that I would publish the book myself. This was a time when self-publishing as we know it today was non-existent. My husband was initially sceptical of the idea and wondered where the funds would come from. However, when he saw my resolve and the fact that I was willing to break my fixed deposit to give shape to my dream, he supported me wholeheartedly. With all my savings devoted to the cause, I set out to publish my book.

My work so far had allowed me to not step out of home, but I was entering new territory now. Having the book printed meant sitting with the printers for long hours, working on the layout and design of the book. While printers line up at the publishing house I run today, looking for work, in those days they refused to take up my project without the payment being made to them in advance. The logistics were also stacked against me. We had one car at that time, which my husband used to commute to his workplace. For my in-laws, seeing their daughter-in-law commuting by public transport in Delhi, at odd hours, making rounds at the printers, wasn't an easy adjustment. By this time, my personal responsibilities had also increased as our son had been born by then. However, I tried to juggle all these roles to the best of my abilities—not wanting to let any one aspect suffer at the cost of the other.

After a lot of effort, my first book, *Vegetarian Wonders*, was printed and ready. While my husband was very proud of my achievement, he still recalls the far-from-encouraging expression on his mother's face on seeing the book. That, I think, was the nature of the times, when women's involvement in the work arena wasn't appreciated. Fortunately, we have come a long way today, and there are far more opportunities for women to make their mark in the workspace.

Coming back to my book: printing it was only half the battle won, as I had no means to distribute the book. Then started the numerous rounds I made to distributors, till one of them agreed to stock my book. If I had thought that this would be the end of my perils, I couldn't be further away from the truth—even after six months of the book being available with the distributor, it didn't sell well. I could have read this as a sign to focus on doing what I did best—run my household—but I wanted to delve deep into the issue and figure out what I could do to improve my offering.

It was during one such brainstorming session that I realized that the issue was that I was simply going with the tide. That while my recipes were good, I was following the format set by other cookbook writers of the time.

I decided then to focus on one ingredient, instead of having a book covering a broad spectrum.

Thus was born the idea of *Paneer All the Way*, a book that would focus only on paneer as the main ingredient to whip up different delicacies. The time was right for this book, as paneer was the only treat available for vegetarians in those days; ingredients like asparagus, broccoli and baby corn hadn't quite made their appearance in the markets yet. What I also did was to print the book in a small size that was handy, so it was easier to refer to it while cooking. Priced at Rs 69, I printed 3000 copies of the book and gave it to the distributor. This time, to my delight, within ten days of printing the book, I received a request from the distributor to give him another 5000 copies. I realized how important it was to carve out one's own niche. In fact, since then, I have made it a point not to read any other cookbook as the style and the format could subconsciously influence me.

After this success, I went on to write twelve books targeting different niches, all of which did very well. However, the distributor felt that the market for cookbooks was saturated, and that I must now sit back and rest on my laurels. I was far from convinced. It was around this time that I visited the Frankfurt Book Fair, and was awed to see the sheer range of titles and the quality of printing. I knew then that I had to listen to my own instincts rather than be influenced by what people's perceptions of the cookbook market were. Today, I have over 600 books to my credit with millions of readers—a feat made possible on account of the invaluable lessons I learnt early on in my career.

Once I started to earn my own money through the sales of my books, I decided to take my cooking classes one step further. It had started becoming increasingly difficult to manage them from home. I set up the Nita Mehta Cooking Academy, a professional school with state-of-the-art equipment. As someone who knew the creative aspect of the business and had no formal training with regard to the management side, I did face my share of setbacks. With limited understanding of the books of accounts, in the early times, I have had instances of employees trying to take advantage of my naivety. However, I never stopped learning and this has stood me in good stead throughout my career. My academy continued to flourish and, over a period of time, I took to the franchising route to scale up its operations further.

In retrospect, if I had to identify the biggest milestone in my career, it perhaps would be when, at the age of eighteen, my son expressed his desire to join my business. I must confess that most people discouraged him, some even openly making fun of him, stating that as a man he would not want to be associated with the business of cooking. Most people were of the opinion that opting for an MBA would be a far better alternative for him. But he stood firm in his decision, for he could clearly visualize that a lot could be done to take the book-publishing aspect of the business ahead. Together, we set up a publishing house of our own, which, besides publishing cookbooks, now also publishes children's books. My experience and his vision quickly became a winning combination, and books such as *Flavours of Indian Cooking*—I did the content and he worked on the look and feel—went on to win the Best Asian Cookbook Award at the Versailles World Cookbook Fair in 1999. In fact, post his retirement, my husband has also started taking a keen interest in the business and we have been exploring new avenues together.

In my long career, there has been enough times when I have second-guessed my own abilities, more so because I did not have any formal degree that equipped me to run a large business. I have often been guilty of undermining myself, thinking that cooking savouries as a homemaker was one thing, developing it into a full-fledged business was quite another. In every situation where I didn't have faith in myself, my family has stood behind me like a rock.

One instance that immediately comes to my mind is when, early on in my career, I was invited to give a demo to about 800 people in Indore. While I was already running my classes at the time, I was extremely nervous about addressing such a large audience. I remember my son boosting my confidence and pushing me to step out of my comfort zone. The same was true when, after his involvement in the business, we decided to set up a fine-dining restaurant called 'Kelong' in Ludhiana. I clearly was a home cook and had no professional training. I was, therefore, apprehensive about running a full-scale restaurant. It was with my son's encouragement that I set out to enhance my learning and picked up the tricks of the trade from the chefs employed in the restaurant. I firmly believe there is only one way to live: to learn and to reinvent. That, by far, has been my biggest life lesson. This, and the fact that with confidence you can achieve just about anything! Simple things like learning how to operate a computer, which comes easily to today's young entrepreneurs, is something that I had to learn painstakingly, but I never shied from embracing change. I could have restricted myself to running my offline classes alone and chosen not to reinvent my business. However, in these days of YouTube and Google, if I hadn't put my recipes and cooking shows on the digital medium, it wouldn't have been the wisest of decisions.

As a homemaker-turned-entrepreneur, I am often asked how other homemakers can begin their start-up journey. I have just one piece of advice to give: do what your heart says and have faith in yourself. If you listen to your heart, the chances of you giving the project your 100 per cent are extremely high and that can lead you to success. Passion, hard work and sincerity, in my mind, are the biggest enablers of success in a start-up.

One other thing that holds back homemakers, I feel, is the fear of a skewed work-life balance. To that, I can only say that as long as you have your priorities in place, you have nothing to fear. With technology on your side, there is a lot you can do today. Among other things, working from a remote location is a possibility now, which wasn't available even a couple of years ago. All you need to do is shed your fears and rise to your potential. Of course, it is extremely important to have a support structure in place by way of your family. But, even there, it is important to remember that support is never one-sided. Today, if I can proudly say that my son and my husband have stood by me through thick and thin, it is also because in pursuing my own career I have never neglected my familial duties.

I, for one, am happy that I have lived a full life without any regrets. Today, besides running my enterprise, I absolutely adore cooking for my grandchildren and, of course, I simply love to eat out. It is a different matter that not many enjoy eating out with me as even there my mind's ticking to see which ingredients have worked for the dish and which haven't!

Life Lessons

✓ Learning is a never-ending journey. We have to constantly keep learning and reinventing.
✓ With confidence, you can achieve anything.

✓ Do what your heart says and always place faith in yourself.

✓ Passion, hard work and sincerity enable success.

✓ Homemakers may fear that stepping into an entrepreneurial role could mean that they will neglect their families. This isn't necessarily true. With proper time management, it is possible to run both your home and enterprise successfully.

4

Veena Kumaravel

~

Chief executive officer, Naturals Beauty Salon India Private Limited that has a turnover of over Rs 250 crore

Moment of Truth: Losses in the family business demanded that she don the entrepreneurial hat.

Starting a business venture after being a homemaker for nearly eight years without any formal training, that too when the family business is floundering, requires great courage and determination, both of which Veena Kumaravel has in spades. Her true contribution to women's entrepreneurship, however, lies in creating an over Rs 250-crore business empire from scratch, while ushering in a beauty revolution and shaping the salon industry as we know it today. She started off with a single salon in Chennai, and now her chain boasts of over 550 salons spread across the country. Today, the rock-solid partnership of Veena and C.K. Kumaravel (her husband actively joined the business after winding up his previous business of manufacturing hair-care products), provides financial emancipation to a whole generation of women—Naturals has a marked preference for women franchisee partners.

A Beautiful Life

'The most beautiful thing you can wear is confidence.'
—Blake Lively, actor

I was born and brought up in Chennai, and spent most of my life within the confines of this beautiful and homely city. Hailing from an upper-middle-class business family, I was blessed with a very happy and comfortable childhood. My grandfather and uncle from my mother's side are reputed doctors, and even though there was no overt pressure on any of us to take up any particular profession, we did feel the weight of expectations. My dream, however, was always to start something of my own, albeit in a small way. I often dreamt of running a playschool or even a small boutique. However, as was the norm, marriage followed soon after I completed my studies.

My husband, C.K. Kumaravel, hails from a business family—they launched Velvette, India's first sachet shampoo, in the late 1970s. Post marriage, I got busy settling down into my new family, and later, I got even busier once I started a family of my own. Often, however, I would find myself itching to do something more than just my familial duties. When my husband broke away from his family business and started out on his own to set up Nature Care Products, I would walk into his office as often as I could and do whatever I could to help him out in his new operations. While I had the full support of my husband in my pursuits, the home front still remained my main priority.

I had been a homemaker for almost eight years, busy with my two kids before I took the plunge into active entrepreneurship. The idea took root when my husband's business, while initially making profits, started to run into losses after it diversified, entered new markets and started manufacturing new products. There was clearly a need for an alternative business model. This was also the time when my children had started going to school and did not need me around all the time. Both of us felt that the time was right for me to strike out on my own and, based on how things worked out, my husband could join my business later.

Despite coming from a business family, I did not have any training when it came to managing an enterprise. It took us a while to zero in on a business idea. Since there was ample space at home, I first toyed with the idea of setting up a playschool. However, the idea of opening a salon that could provide the average Indian a luxurious experience at an affordable price really excited me. Moreover, it also fitted in with our plans synergistically, since my husband was in the business of hair-care products. I realized that while the middle class was growing at a rapid pace, there were hardly any salons to cater to this burgeoning category. There were the high-end luxury salons within five-star hotels on one end and there were small salons operating out of homes on the other.

Through personal experience, I knew how cumbersome the entire process was if you had to schedule an appointment at one of the five-star hotel salons. Not only did you have to book it much in advance, if you happened to be late by even a couple of minutes, your appointment was summarily cancelled and you had to go through the entire process again. Due to the sheer expense and effort involved in going to these luxury salons, their clientele was restricted to the moneyed upper class alone. There were virtually no salons that allowed the average Chennaiite to pamper herself without making a dent in her savings. The fact that I happened to know of a lady who had worked at the Taj salon and was keen to branch out on her own meant that I had a competent person available to steer the operations.

The major issue, however, was funding. While we hear of a lot of financial schemes for women entrepreneurs,

I realized that, on the ground, getting a loan was far from easy. In hindsight, it wasn't just because I was a woman venturing into unchartered territory, it also had a lot to do with the fact that the beauty business wasn't well established at the time and the idea of investing as much as Rs 30 lakh in a salon seemed unviable to banks. It was then that I decided to reach out to friends and family, who more than rose to the occasion and extended financial help.

Thus began the search for a place. I chose a prime location in Chennai, Khader Nawaz Khan Road, to launch the first Naturals salon. This was in the year 2000; today, of course, it is regarded as the high street in Chennai. It took more than six months to set up the entire salon as all the equipment was imported. As I look back, those indeed were difficult times. On the one hand, the line of creditors outside my husband's office was steadily growing, while on the other, we were borrowing heavily to set up the salon. In fact, I am often asked if I wasn't terrified at the time to take up the entrepreneurial mantle, especially since we were seeing a business enterprise steadily going south. The fact is, at the time, I did not see myself setting up a large enterprise. It was meant to be one salon, so I knew that the risk was limited, but if it worked well it would give us enough to run our household comfortably. While we may have been in debt, this clearly was not the time to let fear reign. Besides, I was totally convinced about the value proposition offered by the salon, and was willing to invest whatever time and effort was required to make it succeed.

I left no stone unturned to popularize the place; whether it meant leaving free vouchers at neighbourhood shops to bring in more footfall or introducing innovative services, like the hitherto unknown fruit facial to pamper one's skin. I had to work towards promoting the salon and also towards introducing the concept of people making frequent visits to one—so far, clients used to go to salons only on special occasions. The additional challenge was in sourcing trained manpower. Since there were very few salons back then, it was difficult to find trained people. This, in turn, meant that I had to keep hiring enthusiastic newbies and invest in their training before they could finally start working at the salon. And if they left, it meant I had to repeat the whole cycle again. I remember spending long hours in the salon in those days, not wanting to let a shortage of funds or skilled people force us into taking shortcuts with our customers. More than profit, my aim was to make women feel good about themselves—typically involved with children and families, women often don't give themselves too much importance.

Long hours at the salon also meant a lot of juggling on the home front, although I was lucky that my parents lived close by and they could take care of my children in those early days. Sure, there were days of guilt at not being able to spend as much time with my kids, but with the support of my family I could juggle both roles. In fact, I often meet homemakers who want to set out on their own, but fear that they may not be able to achieve a healthy work-life balance. My experience says that with a good support system, you can manage both—maybe not very comfortably, but you certainly can if you stretch yourself. Also, as the business settles down, your work becomes more flexible, which enables you to spend quality time with your children. Most importantly, however, I feel that the gratification of seeing your children grow up into independent adults in whose eyes you see flashes of pride for your own achievements is simply beyond compare.

Coming back to those initial years, I must confess that despite my efforts, I encountered a loss of over Rs 10 lakh in the first year. Unperturbed, I went on to introduce a number of innovative services—such as a mobile salon, which we could take to the suburbs to cater to those people who couldn't come to Khader Nawaz Khan Road. We also introduced a dial-a-beautician service, where we used to go to customer's homes and offer beauty services. All of this gave us a lot of visibility and publicity.

However, despite all of this, while we were able to cut our losses, we still made a loss of Rs 5 lakh and Rs 2 lakh in years two and three respectively. Clearly, I was running out of resources. My husband had also wound up his previous business by this time and was now involved with Naturals.

We were advised by everyone, including our auditors, to shut down this business. In fact, my mother-in-law was keen that she speak to my husband's brothers, so that he could be taken into their fold and could start earning a steady salary. The only fact that kept us going was that the losses were decreasing with each year, which gave us hope that we were on the right path. It was only in the fourth year that the salon finally made a profit. That was the time we thought of expanding our chain and opening more outlets. Expanding the operations, however, meant a further infusion of funds. We approached numerous banks, only to meet with rejection each time. It was ultimately in our fifty-fourth attempt that we encountered a bank manager who was open-minded enough to appreciate the merit of our idea and he agreed to fund our expansion plans.

The funding helped us open more branches in quick succession. Naturals was by now a chain with five salons in Chennai. I finally felt that my faith in the business was vindicated, and I was seeing our vision translating into reality after a long and hard struggle.

My husband and I felt that the way forward from here was to adopt the franchisee model. I was fascinated by British businesswoman and human rights activist Anita Roddick and the way she had managed to expand The Body Shop from a single small store to a global franchise in just a few years. In fact, I was very interested in bringing this model to India, and during a trip to London, I even managed to arrange a visit to The Body Shop factory to meet Anita. At the time, however, Anita and her team were not sure if India was ready for a concept store like The Body Shop. This was before we started Naturals. Today, of course, The Body Shop has made its presence felt in the big metro cities and is moving from strength to strength.

We started to advertise our expansion plans, inviting franchisees on a pan-India basis. While 300-odd people responded to the advertisement, we could identify only three who could be seriously considered. We made two interesting discoveries in the process. The first was that since we had no salon outside Chennai, it meant that people from other parts of the country did not know anything about Naturals and were therefore hesitant about investing in the venture. Secondly, even within Chennai, we were only known in the pockets where our salons were based, which limited our ability to attract potential partners. This clearly was a setback in our bid to develop the business. We were forced to go back to the drawing board and during one brainstorming session we hit upon the idea of partnering with friends and family. We knew instinctively that we could turn it into a win-win proposition. Our family and friends already knew that the business was steadily increasing in revenue and, hence, agreed to the idea of partnering with us. I first broached the idea to my close cousin in Coimbatore; she was enthusiastic from the word go and we decided to enter into a fifty-fifty partnership model. The costs and profits for the salon would be divided equally between Naturals and her. This is how the sixth Naturals salon came up in Coimbatore. Apart from splitting 50 per cent of the costs involved in setting up a Naturals salon, we also helped our partners by providing them with skilled manpower as well as with promoting the salon in the neighbourhood. The success of this partnership led to similar agreements with other members of the extended family and our friends' circle, and we were back on the expansion track with Naturals salons mushrooming all over south India in quick succession. Soon, we started getting offers for partnerships from all over India. After we had crossed the twenty-five-salon mark in 2008, we decided that this was a good time to adopt the franchisee model. This time around, the response was thunderous and we were able to double the number of salons. Today, we are no longer only a south India–based brand—over 500 of our salons now exist across the country.

The main reason I am so passionate about this industry is that I see it as a powerful tool to empower women. Our partnership and franchisee model has helped so many women step out of their homes and become the breadwinners of their families as beauty care comes naturally to us. It gives me a great sense of satisfaction when I see women all across India embracing the concept of not just being beautiful in their own skin but also making a living out of it. Today, we even run academies to train beauticians—many of whom end up working with us. When I had started out, running salons wasn't a sought-after profession. I feel heartened by the fact that the perception is slowly changing. Today, we have graduates wanting to enrol in our training, which bodes well for the future of this industry and for women in India.

The most important thing for women entrepreneurs, I feel, is to not let your fears and guilt stop you from living your dream. If you are passionate about something, then you should definitely pursue it. There is no wishing away the guilt of a working mother, but I feel it is nothing compared to the guilt you are likely to feel when you reach a certain age and look back at your life to see that you have not accomplished what you set out to do. Of course your children and family need your support, but you can offer it without being physically present at home twenty-four hours a day, seven days a week. Besides, today there are enough opportunities where you can work remotely and still be as effective. My experience tells me that once you start doing something, you will find that you have support from various quarters. Your strong desire to make everything work will, in turn, work for you.

Every so often, as women, we make the mistake of either waiting for the right time to start something new or, having taken the leap, we lose our nerve when the going gets tough. Any business needs at least three to four years to stabilize, and you have to give yourself that much time and make that effort to sustain your dream and passion. The early time can prove to be difficult, but it is only when you start thinking of the enormity of the problem that you start getting pulled down by it. As long as you do something that inspires you, you will automatically give it your 100 per cent. Commercial success is bound to follow, although it shouldn't be your sole purpose of starting a business. The other issue that often plagues us as women entrepreneurs is that we tend to seek validation from other people. The path to entrepreneurship, however, demands that you be self-motivated, and not look out for external appreciation and encouragement beyond a point.

As for my own life, Naturals has been a game-changer. From having started out as a homemaker, not only have I turned into an entrepreneur, but my husband and I have also moved from being life partners to partners at work. While we have our work areas clearly defined based on our individual competencies, the brand benefits from our shared vision. Having grown up alongside the business, my children have also had a ringside view of things. My daughter was three when I started the first salon. I remember taking her with me when the salon was being designed and she would spend long hours watching the whole business come to life. Now that it is time for my children to decide their future, I am happy seeing them spread their wings and build identities of their own. With my son looking to carve his place in the food business and my daughter studying hotel management abroad, my children seem to be in no hurry to take over the family mantle. The decision of whether to join the business or not is entirely their own and, both as a mother and as an entrepreneur, I am happy to see them create a unique space for themselves—just as they are happy to see me take wings and fly.

Life Lessons

- ✓ You start getting weighed down by the problem only if you start thinking of the enormity of it.
- ✓ Never give up easily. Even if the business is failing, have confidence in yourself that if not this then something else will work.
- ✓ If you do something that inspires you, you will automatically work harder to see it succeed. Money is bound to follow.
- ✓ The most important thing for women entrepreneurs is to not let your fears and guilt stop you from living your dream.
- ✓ If you are passionate about something, then you should definitely pursue it.
- ✓ The working mother's guilt does exist, but it is nothing compared what you are likely to feel when you look back at your life and see your dreams lying unfulfilled.

✓ Your family needs your support, but you can offer them this support even without being present at home all the time.

✓ As women, we make the mistake of waiting for the right time to start a business or we lose our nerve when the going gets tough.

✓ It is necessary to give yourself and your business enough time to succeed.

✓ Entrepreneurship demands that we be motivated from within, and not look for external appreciation and encouragement.

5

Patricia Narayan

~

Director, Sandeepha chain of restaurants that has a turnover of Rs 7 crore

Moment of Truth: The thought of ending her life as she was in an abusive marriage, and then choosing to live for the sake of her unborn child.

Forced to turn to entrepreneurship on account of debilitating life conditions—an early marriage, an abusive, alcoholic husband and two young children—Patricia Narayan's story is far from ordinary. From trying to rebuild her life by operating a small food stall at Marina Beach to owning a chain of restaurants, hers is a tale of towering willpower in the face of glaring loss. Little surprise then that on days that she feels overwhelmed by her life, this winner of the Devi Award (2016) and FICCI Entrepreneur of the Year Award (2010) dips in to her own challenging journey to inspire herself.

Standing Tall

'If you don't like something, change it; if you can't change it, change your attitude.'
—Maya Angelou, American poet and civil rights activist

The first seventeen years of my life seem like a dream to me now; they were undoubtedly my happiest years, spent in blissful ignorance of the many struggles that lay ahead of me. If I could turn the clock back, I would love to become that carefree sixteen-year-old again, living an idyllic life in a big joint family in Chennai. The eldest of three children, I was the apple of my father's eye. My mother, a working woman herself, had big dreams for my future. Dreams that I was not destined to fulfil.

Growing up, I had no burning ambition to be successful or be anyone of importance. If I had one passion, it had to be food. Trying out different dishes and serving them to people came naturally to me. Life indeed did come full circle as my childhood hobby became my bread and butter in my later years.

I met my future husband in my second year of college, and my carefree existence took an unexpected turn. I remember how I couldn't resist crossing the street to watch the sheer magic of *chhole*–puris being prepared at the restaurant located across the road from my college. The fact that I could see how a commercial kitchen worked drew me like a moth to a flame. A small stove at home does not really inspire you to experiment, but watching the equipment in the restaurant kitchen work was like witnessing poetry in motion. It so happened that the restaurant was supervised by a young man, whose family owned the place. Thirteen years older than me, he appeared extremely worldly wise and I was taken in by his charming manners. In hindsight, it was probably the fact that his family owned a restaurant that attracted me to him more than anything else. Our friendship grew and, before I knew it, barely three months since we met, we were getting married. I was only seventeen then, not even of legal marriageable age and, of course, I still had to complete my graduation.

My parents obviously did not agree with this decision, so I did the next best thing: I got married without their knowledge; much less, their consent. Even in my naivety, I knew that this information would come as a big blow to them; so I thought I would share the news with them only after I graduated from college. I believed that the fact that I would also be eighteen by then would help soften the blow. My husband, who was in agreement with this decision till before we got married, changed his stance subsequently and began to put pressure on me to tell my parents of my marital status, failing which he threatened to tell them himself. I had to break the news to them within three months of my marriage. Till today, this is my greatest regret—that I totally ruined their hopes for me and their happiness. My father was especially heartbroken to see me take such an irresponsible decision. Left with no choice, my family arranged for a formal wedding, but thereafter cut off all ties with me.

My rosy life came to an abrupt end with this one step: a step I had taken with virtually no understanding of its implications and consequences. We rented a small flat, and this brought me face-to-face with the harsh realities of life in ways I could never have imagined. It was only after I started living with my husband that I saw a side of him that I could not have even envisaged during our courtship period. I realized that he was an alcoholic and was into drugs. It was too late for the enormity of my mistake to sink in. I was aware that I had brought this misery upon myself. While I spent the first couple of months trying to help him overcome his drinking problems, among other things, I soon realized that, like me, he had already reached the point of no return.

The only reward I got for my efforts was to get beaten up by him. I was already struggling to make my marriage work when I realized that I was pregnant, and I simply had no means to support myself. My husband could not hold a job down on account of his many vices. The sense of hopelessness that pervaded me made me even consider ending my life. Only the thought of the unborn child growing within me stopped me from taking any drastic step. The thought of losing my child also made me realize the trauma my parents would undergo on losing me, and I could not subject my parents to that kind of pain. Clearly the only options available were either to surrender to my circumstances or stand up and fight. I chose the latter.

Because I was barely educated, I knew that finding a job would not be easy. To support myself, I started doing the first thing I thought I could. In this case it was making artificial flowers out of satin. They came out so beautifully that the first lot sold out in no time. Soon, orders started pouring in. While business was good, I was a one-person army and could do only so much. I had no machines to help me with the cutting and pasting; it was just me sitting through the night making the roses and pasting them together. There were nights when my spine would refuse to straighten, what with all the work I had put in. Despite this, my daily income was meagre. I felt overwhelmed as I had no knowledge of business, and no way of knowing how

I could employ people and expand this into a profitable business model. The earnings were simply not enough to meet my needs, especially since a part of it needed to be put back into the business. I knew I had to look for something more scalable than this. It was during this time that my thoughts turned towards my passion—cooking.

I had a natural flair for making jams, pickles and squashes, so I decided to try and sell them commercially. The first lot got sold out instantly and demands started pouring in for more. My limitations came into play again—I was working alone, using a small stove in my kitchen—and there was only so much that I could prepare even if I worked twenty-four hours a day, seven days a week. The lack of guidance and my own inexperience in running a business limited my ability to take it to the next level. Today, armed with all the business knowledge I have gained in the last few years, I can think of ten different ways to scale up the business; but, back then, as an inexperienced youngster, my options seemed pretty limited.

So there I was—penniless, with two children in tow by now and a husband who simply couldn't hold down a job, much less provide for us. Seeing that I was stuck in such a situation, my father decided to open his house to my family. I count my father and myself lucky—since he worked night shifts, he didn't have to see the brutal side of my husband, when, unable to handle his cravings at night, he would physically abuse me.

I knew that I could not be a burden on my father and I continued to look for avenues to work. This was when fate intervened. The government was leasing out kiosks in public areas on the condition that the stall owners employ handicapped children. I jumped at the offer, determined to set up a food kiosk on Marina Beach. Training handicapped children to prepare and serve tea and coffee was the easy part, the more tedious process involved getting the approvals required to set up the stall. I had zero experience in handling government agencies. It was by no means an easy ride; the process of getting all the necessary permissions took me more than a year. Beaches come under the jurisdiction of the Public Works Department. I remember walking into their office, climbing up the stairs to the eighth floor with an infant in my arms, trying to get my application approved. I managed to meet the Secretary after a day-long wait only to be re-directed to the relevant division. It was after I pursued my request for over a year that I was given the permission to set up a stall.

Without wasting any time, I set to work preparing the savouries so I could set up the kiosk the next morning. I was the first one to set up a stall at Anna Square on Marina Beach and was lucky in the sense that I started out with virtually no competition. The only stalls that existed back then used to sell cigarettes and tea. My stall, on the other hand, was filled with savouries like cutlets, *bajji*s, samosas, fresh juice, tea and coffee.

What can I say about that first morning when I set up my stall on the beach? I started out filled with excitement, and I had prepared a whole range of eatables that I hoped would sell out. As the day ended, however, my total sale amounted to exactly 50 paisa from the single cup of coffee I had sold. Imagine my dismay and disappointment when I came back home with only 50 paisa to show for all my effort and hard work. I was in tears—all the food and money had gone down the drain, not to mention all my effort. That day, I learnt my first business lesson—always cook limited portions to minimize wastage. While I set foot in my stall with a lot of reservation the next day, it being a weekend, I was in for a complete surprise as my food and drinks flew off the counter. There was no turning back from there. Each day I experimented with something new and learnt a new business lesson. Marina Beach became my MBA school and I picked up many invaluable lessons there.

Each day—from 3 p.m. till 11 p.m.—I would be at the beach stall, come what may, giving it my all. We did average business during the weekdays, but during the weekends and holidays we really made a killing. Little by little, we kept growing and as the business grew so did my knowledge of catering to consumer tastes. This slow but steady pace of growth was good for me in hindsight, as I did not have the resources or the capital to support a massive growth spurt.

While my revenue was increasing, the money was still not enough to keep up with the swelling demands at home. My children were growing up and so were their needs. Added to this was the fact that my husband's demands had begun to increase along with my expanding income. Thankfully, my children were under my mother's able care, so I did not have to worry too much on that front. I had to come back to the drawing board, to think about how I could make ends meet. As I sat thinking of various alternatives, it dawned on me that while I was busy with the stall from 3 p.m. onwards, my mornings were relatively free. I started looking for work that I could do exclusively in the mornings.

As luck would have it, it was around this time that the chairman of the Slum Clearance Board, a regular at my stall, impressed with my food, suggested that I run their office canteen. Needless to say, I immediately jumped at the offer and took up the catering assignment at the Slum Clearance Board. The good part about government offices is that you work for fixed hours—I used to be in office from 8 a.m. to 5 p.m. and from there, I would go directly to the beach to set up my stall. The additional income helped me tremendously, so when some of my regular customers at the beach suggested that I open the stall in the morning as well to cater to the morning walkers, I immediately decided to act on the suggestion. My day now started even earlier: I would be at the stall from 4 a.m. to

8 a.m., serving fresh juices to morning walkers. From there, I would go straight to the office of the Slum Clearance Board till 5 p.m. My third shift of the day would begin after that, with me selling hot bajjis and samosas on the beach in the evening. Despite my hectic schedule, I never felt the need to complain simply because I loved what I was doing. Another thing I ensured from the start was to practise strict time management. A big part of my success can be contributed to these two factors: it was my passion that sustained me during tough times and my excellent time management skills that ensured that I remained on track.

There were both pluses and minuses of running a catering business twenty-five years ago. While I had no degree or background in hotel management, fortunately, there was very little competition. Being a woman though was sometimes held against me. I still remember being told by the chairman of the National Institute of Port Management, where I had gone to apply for a catering assignment, that it was not a housewife's job. Incensed by this statement, I told him that I could prove that I could do the job just as well, but he wouldn't hear of it and brought the meeting to an end as he thought that women were only fit to work in their kitchens at home. The same company was, however, forced to call me back a couple of months later as the man they had employed for the job could not do justice to it. I remember taking charge of the kitchen overnight and getting to work the very next morning, catering to 500 young recruits who would come to the canteen tired and hungry after their rigorous physical activities.

My hard work, pluck and a little bit of luck opened up many more doors for me and I took up catering assignments at many other institutes like the National Institute of Food Management. From there, I started pitching to other government universities and colleges, and I landed more assignments, including the merchant navy college in Chennai. My workday remained the same: I was working from 4 a.m. to 11 p.m., the only difference was that I was now catering to far more people. Although I had a team working for me, I made sure I remained involved at every location to ensure the quality of our food and service remained high. I also decided to incorporate my catering organization and started having a more professional, institutionalized approach towards the whole business of catering. Even though the business was doing well, I did not let go of my stall at the beach. I would still see to it that I was at the beach in the evenings, running my stall.

Around that time, I also started dabbling in the restaurant business. My first restaurant was quite a novelty in those days on account of its open kitchen. By now, I had finally moved out of my parents' home into an independent house. My children were growing up and it was time to plan for their future. I loved watching the students at the merchant navy college in their smart uniforms and knew that the job came with a good pay cheque. But what really appealed to me was the fact that the officers were expected to be at sea for three months followed by three months off to spend time with their families. Since there are no fixed timings in the kind of work I did, it left me with very little time for my family. I, therefore, wanted my son to have what I had missed out on. Even though he was very keen on joining the catering business, I persuaded him to join the merchant navy college instead. After finishing his studies in London, he came back and joined the merchant navy. It gave me immense joy to see him doing well. My husband had passed away by then after a fairly difficult life battling his addictions. It was around this time that my daughter's wedding was fixed and it was with a lot of happiness that I went about preparing for it. I was buoyed by the fact that both my children were settling down in life and I was planning my own retirement in another five years, with the possibility of spending time with my grandchildren. However, fate had reserved its cruellest blow for me.

It was a phone call that brought my life to a complete halt. I was told that my daughter had been in an accident. While it took me over two hours to reach the hospital where she was supposedly being rushed, there was no sign of her even though the accident site was only twenty minutes away. Finally, I saw a couple of taxis pull into the hospital and, for a moment, I was hopeful that perhaps my daughter and son-in-law had survived the crash with only minor injuries. Imagine my utter horror when their bodies and those of two close relatives were dragged out from the taxis. I broke down completely. I had spoken to my daughter just a little while before she met with the accident, and she had told me that she was on her way home and that I should keep her favourite food ready. She had only been married for a month and her life had ended even before it had begun. To think that her body was also treated so badly left me inconsolable. At that very instant I decided that I would start an ambulance service to ensure that the dead were treated with the dignity they deserved.

I have always been a very goal-oriented person. Be it my work or something that the children wanted, I have always set a goal and worked tirelessly to achieve it. Only that this time, it was a goal that had arisen out of my deepest loss. The accident took place on 31 May 2004, just six months before my daughter's birthday. I decided that by her birthday I would have the ambulance service in place. It was a Herculean task to procure an ambulance and get it refitted to carry dead bodies. A lot of paperwork and governmental approvals were required. I used to do the two-hour commute almost every day to get the required approvals and to oversee the work being done. I was determined that the service should start in my daughter's name on her birthday from the very place where she had died. It's been thirteen years since my daughter passed away and since then the ambulance service has been operational. Of course, I still ask god why he had to inflict such a terrible punishment on me; I would have started the ambulance service even if he had sent me a message in some other way that did not involve the brutal loss of my daughter.

My next goal was to ensure that the tombstones for the four deceased were erected before their first death anniversary. If I had not taken these two tasks upon myself, I might perhaps have broken down completely. They kept me focused, as there was no way I was going to let my daughter's death go in vain. But once these two goals were accomplished, I was left terribly alone with a sense of total emptiness and the deepest depression. I lost interest in work, in just about every aspect of life. I would sit all day staring at the walls of my home; walls that were covered with photographs of my daughter, where she seemed so full of life. The next few years flew by like this. It was as if I was living in a daze.

My son could not bear to see me living alone like this, so he left his job in the merchant navy and joined me. He took over the day-to-day operations of the business, while I sank deeper and deeper into depression. I stopped meeting anyone or going out; even simple conversations became difficult for at the slightest provocation I would start sobbing uncontrollably. I simply could not make peace with what had happened.

Time, as they say, is a great healer. While I wouldn't go so far as to say that it healed me, it definitely did pull me up enough to be able to go through the motions of life, albeit without any zeal or fervour. In a sense, I received the FICCI award at a very opportune moment. I was living in a vacuum till then, where I had bottled up all my grief. When they came looking for me, desiring to feature my entrepreneurial story, I initially refused to let them interview me. But they were very persistent and persuasive. Once I opened up, I realized how much grief and anger I had stored inside me. Once the article was published, I was flooded with calls, letters and mails from people who wanted to share their story with me. There were people who wrote to me saying they were going through a similar loss and were finding it difficult to overcome their misery. It was then that I realized that I could be of service to people going through the same kind of suffering. I knew the pain of loss and could prove to be a living example of how not to let it take over your life. Today, I am no longer afraid of sharing my story; in fact, I want more and more people to know my story so that they can see that there is indeed light at the end of the tunnel.

I now lead a seemingly normal life; I have taken up new corporate assignments and have gone back to working from 5.30 a.m. to 11 p.m. Of course, the questions and the grief remain; they are a permanent part of me now. I, however, take solace in the fact that my daughter is in a much better place and that I will join her there one day. It grieves me to hear of young kids passing away; at these times, I am thankful to god that I had my daughter with me for twenty-one years at least. I have chosen to be positive and to count my blessings, instead of being miserable about my sorrows.

It was on my son's suggestion that we started to run several restaurants in the name of my daughter. We had already been associated with a very prestigious hotel chain in Chennai for the last ten years and we decided that it was time to put our experience to good use. I stood by my son's side as the Sandeepha chain of restaurants was born. The business is now focused mainly on food courts and the company employs over 200 people.

If I was to look back on my professional journey, the one important lesson I learnt is that that you need passion and commitment to succeed. For women seeking to start out on their own, I would strongly advise that you get into something that you really care about. It is only if you are passionate that you will be able to survive the many low points that are bound to come your way. Without passion, you are likely to get buried by the very first failure. The only other thing you need is confidence in your own abilities. Don't worry about the fact that you do not have any prior experience; you will learn as you go along.

As a woman entrepreneur, you are likely to meet many naysayers who will go all out to tell you why you may not succeed. However, the only person who can help you out is yourself. It is necessary to understand yourself and tap into your latent energies. In fact, I did just that when my daughter passed away. I talked myself into coming out of my listless mental state. You can be your own greatest mentor. In my life, whenever I have wanted to do something, I have said it over and over to myself at least a 100 times so that I believe in it. It is clearly a case of mind over matter; all you need to do is train yourself accordingly. People often ask me who my role model in this long and arduous journey has been. Honestly, instead of looking at other people's lives, in times of despair, the only thing I look towards is my own story to draw inspiration for the road ahead. In that sense, I am my own role model.

Even though I have achieved some success, at no point can I say that I have done enough and that I must hang up my boots. Till the time I live, I need to keep going. Along the way, however, if my story can inspire even a single woman to go out and make a life for herself, I would think my life was worthwhile.

Life Lessons

✓ While I did not go to a formal MBA school, Marina Beach taught me many business lessons.

✓ It was my passion that sustained me during tough times and my excellent time management skills that ensured I continued working towards my goal.

✓ It is important to remain positive and count your blessings, instead of being miserable because of your sorrows.

✓ Passion for your work can see you through the many failures that you will encounter.

✓ Unless you love your work, you start looking at your watch and start wondering when you can go home.

✓ Confidence in your own abilities will take you far.

✓ Women entrepreneurs are more likely to meet naysayers who will tell them that they are more likely to fail. It is necessary to have confidence in your own abilities.

✓ Talk to yourself about your goal and tap into your latent energies.

✓ Whenever I have wanted to achieve something, I have said it over and over to myself so that I believe in it.

✓ At all the low points in your life, turn around and see how far you have come in your journey.

✓ If my story can inspire even one woman to go make a life for herself, I would think I have succeeded.

6

Sarada Ramani

~

Founder and president, Computers International, an enterprise mobility services company with a turnover of Rs 50 crore

Moment of Truth: An innocuous remark by her daughter, lamenting Sarada's lack of computer knowledge, sparked her desire to master this unknown beast.

Sarada Ramani's foray into entrepreneurship came fourteen years after playing the homemaker role to perfection—when most professionals have already crossed the mid-way mark in their work life. The push towards reclaiming a lost career came on account of an innocent comment made by her daughter. However, once she took the first step towards entrepreneurship, there has been no stopping this lady whose middle name is optimism. The president of a technology firm, she has not only been honoured with the National Award for being an outstanding woman entrepreneur (2006), she has, in the process, opened doors for many other women to carve out their own space in the male-dominated world of technology.

Ambika Pillai: Beauty that isn't skin-deep

Savita Chhabra: Taking charge

Nita Mehta: Cooking her way into every heart

Veena Kumaravel: 'Naturally' successful

Patricia Narayan: Survivor extraordinaire

Sarada Ramani: The 'IT' woman

Anasuya Gupta: The baton bearer

Jyothi Reddy: A dream journey

Anuradha Pegu: Weaving a strong narrative

Rakhee Vaswani: A recipe for success

Sundeep Bhandal: Beating the odds

Pabiben Rabari: Fusing the old with the new

Decoding Success

'It is never too late to be what you might have been.'
—George Eliot, English poet and novelist

My husband often says that I am like a river that flows with the drift. However, whichever direction I take, I ensure I put my heart and soul into it. Entrepreneurship, like just about everything else in my life, happened quite by accident; and of course I took to it like a fish takes to water. Now when I look back, I feel that perhaps destiny had started preparing me for my entrepreneurial journey right from my childhood.

I grew up in Chennai, and was the eldest of three siblings of working parents. The take-charge attitude so typical of entrepreneurs came early to me. Since the age difference was substantial—six years between my youngest brother and me—my siblings were used to following my lead. In the absence of my parents all day, I learnt to manage on my own, to take initiative and to innovate while taking care of my two younger brothers. As a child though, I never had big dreams about becoming a doctor or an astronaut or anything fancy like that. My dreams were very ordinary: to finish my education, work for a couple of years and then settle down into matrimony. As for being an entrepreneur, there was no conscious thought or desire simply because no one in my close family had ever tried to be one.

I went on to join a bank as a clerk after my graduation, which is where I met my husband. My husband hails from a family of farmers, but he chose to break with tradition. Since both of us happened to belong to the same community, our marriage was blessed by the elders from both sides. Life changed dramatically for me after marriage. While my husband's family lived in Poyyamani village about 30 kms from Tiruchirappalli, I, on the other hand, had been born and brought up in the city. Post marriage, I decided to give up my job to focus on settling in with my new family. While my boss tried to dissuade me from resigning, I was determined as I wanted my married life to proceed smoothly. I moved, bag and baggage, to the village.

Life in the village was a sea change from how I had lived until then; however, I didn't rue the change. While my husband's family welcomed me wholeheartedly, their set-up was quite different. For starters, cooking was done on a mud *chullah*, a bit of a shocker for a city-bred girl like me.

What was also quite jarring was that women were not expected to step out of the house; to the extent that even when an outsider came into the house, the women were supposed to step into the kitchen and come out only when called for. I accepted all of this as a part of their traditions and also for the fact that despite their conservative lifestyle, they respected me for my background and intelligence. Time went by and I went on to have a daughter, and was contented with my world.

By the time my daughter was old enough to start school, we decided to move to Chennai for the sake of her education. Even then, we made it a point to go back to the village every weekend and stay with the family. After a brief stay in Chennai, my husband was posted to Agra. This was also around the time when my second daughter was born. Even though it was a long journey from Agra to our village down south, I made sure that my children celebrated every major festival, be it Diwali or Pongal, with the family.

In these intervening years, my husband continued to encourage me to do something for myself as he believed that I had a lot of potential. When computers first came to the country, he persuaded me to learn the ropes by reskilling myself. I was, however, apprehensive as I felt that I had passed the age of learning and I did not want to step out of my comfort zone. I continued to do a lot of community work though and was happy with the way my life had shaped up.

Things, however, turned on their head when my daughter started to study computers in school. While I helped her out with her homework, when it came to computer science, I drew a blank. My daughter's comment, 'What is this, Amma, you don't know anything about computer science!' hit me like a bolt of lightning. It forced me to step back and re-evaluate my life. I remember wondering that if this little chit of a girl could do it, what was really stopping me from learning it too.

Truth be told, at that time, my motivation to learn was still based on the fact that I should be able to coach her. With this determination, I set out to find some computer classes that would suit my routine. Of course, I did not want to enrol for a year-long course, mainly because I doubted my own ability to stick it out. Also a year-long computer course required an investment of Rs 35,000, which, at that time, amounted to a great deal of money. With two school-going children and only my husband's income sustaining us, it did not feel right to spend so much money on myself. Perhaps I was also plagued by the typical middle-class mentality to save money for the future of my children, while keeping myself at the bottom of the priority list.

Fortunately for me, a newly opened computer centre was offering classes for just Rs 1500 and I decided to enrol there. Other things also worked in my favour: the centre was located close to my children's school and classes were held from 10 a.m. to 1 p.m., which gave me ample time to drop them and pick them up.

I can still recall the batch I studied with: it was a heterogeneous group consisting mostly of middle-aged people like me, as well as a few senior citizens, but none of us had joined the course from a career perspective. The concept was so new back then that the monitor and the keyboard seemed extremely threatening to me. I often feared that I would press a wrong button and the machine would explode in flames. I had even started calculating how much money I might be asked to pay for replacing the computer. After a couple of days, however, my fears started subsiding and I actually started enjoying the fact that I was learning a new skill. After having picked up the basics, I graduated to programming. It was wonderful to see things come alive on the computer screen; the feeling had me hooked.

After this course, I learnt that Microsoft was launching a course on C++ and Visual C++. I went on to enrol in this programme. Unlike my previous group, this one consisted of professionals who were acquiring these skills for career reasons. Of the twenty-member class, only four of us were non-engineers. In my earlier course, I had been way ahead of the class as I was able to pick things up pretty quickly. Here, I found myself struggling and had to put in extra hours just to keep myself going. One thing I have realized, and for which I am eternally grateful, is that if you are keen to learn something, people around you are willing to help. My entire household stood by me like a rock to ensure that I could put in the time and effort required to succeed in class. I used to have a packed schedule back then and everything needed to run like clockwork so I could concentrate on my classes. I used to see the children off and finish all the household work by 10 a.m., after which I would rush to the computer lab to put in a couple of hours of work. At 2 p.m., I would hurry to pick the kids up from school and then, after spending an hour or so with them, I would need to get ready to leave for my class. My children knew that I had very little time, so they would ensure that they did their homework immediately after coming home, so I could leave in peace. My husband, on his part, tried to be home by 5 p.m. to look after the kids and take care of the house. All three of them went out of their way every single day to ensure that I achieved my goal.

My efforts paid off when I finally finished in the top three of my class. This is when I thought to myself that although I had set out with the sole aim of being able to teach my kids, I should put my learning to good use. I had thought that I would be able to get a job with my computer diplomas. I could not have been further away from the truth. My father arranged for an interview with a software firm through someone he knew. Having seen my profile, when the interviewer heard that I was thirty-five years old, he started to shake his head. Very politely, but equally firmly, he told me, 'Amma, I am very sorry, I will not be able to employ you because, as a company policy, we employ engineers up to the age of twenty-four. You are about ten years too late.' This curt statement made it clear to me that my career options as a software programmer were pretty limited.

Determined to not let my skills rust, I turned towards the next best option, i.e., to become a faculty member at a computer training institute. Needless to say, I was the most junior faculty there as I came with no work experience. I also happened be the oldest, which meant that others much younger than me were my seniors in the institute. Since classes mostly happened for two or three hours a day, I started helping out with the administrative work involved in running the centre. I even went to distribute pamphlets as a part of the marketing effort to increase the footfall. I must confess that at my age I used to find it very awkward standing at a bus stop or going to colleges to distribute pamphlets, but I persisted, nevertheless, wanting to do everything I could to make the institute grow from strength to strength. Soon I found myself managing every aspect of the centre without being assigned a formal role.

The company's CEO would visit our branch once a month to go over the operations at the centre and he happened to notice my work during one of his visits. It was he who told me that I had the makings of an entrepreneur and that I could set up a franchise of the office if I so wished. This one statement opened up the floodgates of entrepreneurship in me. Having no business background, however, my family was very much against the idea in the beginning. Eventually, my husband agreed, but it was by no means an easy decision. The franchise fee itself came to approximately Rs 50 lakh and it was a huge investment decision in those times.

Having decided to give it a shot, I started gathering resources to put a project plan in place. Thus began the endless rounds to banks for a loan. The fact that I was a woman without any prior experience in business and that the brand wasn't too well known meant that I had to face rejection from every quarter. Eventually, I had to secure a loan from outside at a higher rate of interest. A similar fate awaited me when I started to look for space to set up operations, as most people were apprehensive of giving the place to a newbie businesswoman, unsure of whether I would actually be able to pay the rent on time. It was with great difficulty that I finally managed to get a place. Years later, I had tears in my eyes as my landlord confided in me that like everyone else he too had his apprehensions about renting out the space to me as if I failed, he had a lot to lose and that he often used to pray for my success. I remember being overwhelmed by his words and being driven even further to succeed.

I started out with a six-member staff and a whole lot of apprehensions as, for the first time, I was responsible for the livelihoods of other people. The one thought that kept me going, however, was that if people had trusted me enough to join my company, I needed to succeed in order to live up to their trust. We started off very promisingly and things went well for a year. It was around this time that I took a big business decision that ended up costing me a lot. I came to know of another franchisee that was looking for an equity partner. In fact, for a while, I had been helping the owner find an equity partner by introducing him to my circle of friends. Eventually, I talked to my husband about investing in the equity partnership myself. I went on to invest Rs 5 lakh, which I had to borrow at a high rate of interest and which put me in debt from the very beginning. I had thought that by leveraging costs between the two centres, I would stand to gain. However, things did not pan out the way I had envisaged. By the end of the year, we were in deep financial trouble—we were not generating the kind of business we had anticipated and debts were mounting. Things were so bad that I felt a surge of relief when the working week ended, as Sunday would mean I could have one day of peace in between the mounting chaos.

Between handing out salaries on time and handling cagey investors, who feared that I would default on their loans, things were getting extremely hard to manage. I was bracing myself for the possibility of shutting down the business to liquidate the assets in order to pay off the debts. This is when fate intervened to give me a new lease of life.

It was at this time that I learnt of a USA-based organization which was looking for an outsourcing partner in India as their current partner was not delivering the kind of quality they wanted. They felt that if there was a dedicated team working only for them, they would be able to control the quality of the output. The director of the company knew my brother and thought that I could extend my training business to run an outsourcing unit. I was initially hesitant because I did not know anything about this business. However, I realized that I had known very little about the training business as well when I first started out. With my brother's help, we were able to negotiate a deal which helped the US company get a better quality job done at a lower price than what they were previously paying, while helping us earn a profit as well.

The initial plan was to use the space as a training centre during the day and as a software development centre at night, which would enable us to share the infrastructure. However, my biggest concern was security of data. In a training centre, rank outsiders had access to the systems and if I used the same systems at night, there were chances of the data being compromised, which could eventually put me in a difficult position. Also most of the computers at the centre were old and had limited functionality. I took two big decisions then, both of which were vehemently opposed by my family. They kept cautioning me against taking more loans when we already had so much accumulated debt. As it turns out, my strong stance at that time helped us build a lasting relationship with our client.

The first decision was to take up a separate space for the software development centre. I, however, ensured that the space was merely utilitarian and did not spend any money on frills. In fact, I did not even allow myself a decent office. I would sit outside the room like a receptionist. The second was that I went about equipping the place with new and faster machines that could help improve our productivity. Both gambles paid off, as we were able to deliver vastly superior quality at less than half the price the client had been paying previously. This was a period of immense learning for me, as I didn't even know what skill sets to look for in the team that needed to be recruited. I remember taking the help of an adviser who gave me the questions that I needed to administer to the candidates and the answers in a separate sheet. In an incident that still makes me laugh, I remember erroneously photocopying both the question and the answer sheet, and nearly handing over both to the candidates.

Despite starting out with knowing virtually nothing about the product, with our hard work and dedication, we soon became one of the most appreciated teams working for the client. Today, of course, we are a world-class entity with clients spread across USA, Canada, South Africa and Australia, and a steady source of revenue as well as zero debt.

Running a business, however, is all about learning a new lesson every day—more so if you happen to be a woman and a first-generation entrepreneur like me. In my long stint as a woman entrepreneur, I have learnt some invaluable lessons. One of them, of course, is the fact that one needs to have a sense of balance between ensuring a healthy bottom line versus chasing the top line. My first experience of debt scarred me forever and the second time around I was determined not to take any risks whatsoever and follow a fairly conservative approach. However, I think excessive focus on the bottom line to the point of ignoring the top line isn't a great strategy for businesses either and it is something that women entrepreneurs can get pulled down by.

Another aspect that I feel women sometimes ignore is that of image management. A valuable lesson that I have learnt is that in business you have to constantly project a larger-than-life image. Sometimes we tend to brush these small concerns aside, thinking that they are unimportant, especially if you are a housewife-turned-entrepreneur like me. Let me give you an example from my early days. When I ran a training centre, I used to go to the houses of my students on weekends to promote the centre. I would take my husband along, more for safety than anything else.

Even though it was my company and my initiative, all the queries would be directed towards my husband and I would find myself simply standing on the sidelines, listening to the conversation. It was only later that I realized that not only do I need to take charge of the conversation but I also need to dress well to create a good first impression. In fact, as women, we need to consciously learn to dedicate time and effort towards our own overall development, instead of relegating ourselves to the bottom of the priority list. I, for one, continued with my education even after starting a business. Today I have MCS and MBA degrees. These qualifications, I feel, add value to my profile and have helped increase my ability to interact with others.

The Achilles heel in the case of women entrepreneurs is also the need to strive for a work-life balance. I think the important thing with regard to this is not to expect perfection from yourself. Early on in my entrepreneurial journey, I had told my daughters that while there could be small aspects of their lives that I may miss out on, there are some non-negotiable aspects that I would always be there for. So while they may not find me at the gates of their school with hot food during their lunch breaks, I would always be there when it came to imparting them with the self-confidence and skills required to take on the world. To fellow women co-workers, I have just one thing to say— learn to live with the working mom's guilt without making it the be-all and end-all of your life.

Lastly, and this applies to all entrepreneurs and not just women entrepreneurs, any business will have its cycle of ups and downs. When you are down and out, don't think of what is not working for you, instead start looking at opportunities that exist and how you can leverage them to grow.

I am proud of what I have been able to achieve over these years. Receiving the Best Woman Entrepreneur of the Country Award in 2006 from the then President of India, Dr A.P.J. Abdul Kalam, was an honour beyond words. I felt truly vindicated that day for all the blood, sweat and tears I had put into building this company. We have received many other awards over the years, all thanks to my wonderful team. My greatest sense of achievement comes from watching my daughters' faces swell with pride when I go up to receive these awards. More than anything else, I feel happy that I have given them the confidence to pursue their dreams. Today my younger daughter is doing her MS in gynaecology and my elder daughter is the country head for a US-based company.

Having received so much, I feel now is my time to give back to the entrepreneurial ecosystem. I am an active participant in forums with a view to encourage dialogue and discussion around the empowerment of women. I want to mentor more and more women, so they can step out of their comfort zone and take up the challenge of building a successful career. I hope that my story inspires at least some of them and gives wings to their dreams.

Life Lessons

✓ When you fail, don't look at what is not working. Instead, look at the opportunities around you and leverage them.

✓ You have to be clear about your priorities and stop expecting perfection from yourself or think that you can be a super mom.

✓ It is important for women to spend time, money and effort on their own development.

✓ In business, you have to constantly project a larger than life image of yourself.

✓ As women entrepreneurs, we sometimes tend to focus more on the bottom line and ignore the top line.

✓ People around you are willing to help you if you want to do something with your life.

✓ The working mom's guilt is bound to exist, but don't allow it to take over your life.

✓ We need to consciously learn to dedicate time and effort towards our own overall development.

7

Anasuya Gupta

~

Chairperson and managing director, CICO Technologies, a key participant in the construction chemicals industry with a turnover of Rs 87 crore

Moment of Truth: Being referred to as '*Annadata*' by the workers after the untimely demise of her husband, which brought her responsibility towards them into sharp focus.

Happy to be a homemaker, Anasuya took over the reins of the family business after her husband's death in 2008, twenty-two years after their wedding. Her children were nineteen and sixteen at the time. Today, she not only leads a specialized chemical company, CICO Technologies, with its Mission 100 (its goal of reaching Rs 100 crore of revenue in the next year and a half), she also has been honoured as a business leader of substance and an outstanding woman contributor in the construction and infrastructure industry. Under her leadership, CICO has won several awards, including best professionally managed company and outstanding company in construction chemicals during the fourth EPC World Award 2013.

Mind over Matter

'Life shrinks or expands in proportion to one's courage.'
—Anaïs Nin, author

My husband, Amit, used to quip often that I succeed in doing a lot of things because ignorance is bliss; I go through situations without worrying about their consequences. Looking back at how life panned out, it seems that he analysed me pretty well.

When he passed away in 2008, our kids were nineteen and sixteen. People often ask me if I saw the end coming, especially because we had spent fifteen years going in and out of hospitals ever since Amit was first diagnosed with renal failure. Strangely enough, I hadn't, because despite there being many episodes of his being really unwell, he bounced back every single time. In spite of his illness and our frequent hospital visits, I can safely say that we didn't lose out on family time. If anything, it brought us much closer together. In fact, we made it a point to give each other enough time—whether it was in the evenings with the children tucked into bed by 7.30 p.m. or whilst we travelled together. I, for one, was very happy being a homemaker all those years. I daresay I took my role pretty seriously. From running the house like clockwork to being in the front row of every function the children had in school, I enjoyed every minute of it.

If I were to look back now, perhaps taking each day as it comes had its genesis in my growing up years—a wholesome childhood spent in Calcutta. My years in convent school, where the focus was on laying a strong value system, made me the person I am today. More than anything else, my childhood was a safe haven that gave me the opportunity to spread my wings, and I did take flight in my own little ways. An outdoorsy person, I played many a sport, including basketball, hockey and cricket. I even went on to represent Bengal in basketball. With my many interests in singing, dancing and theatre, I certainly had my hands full.

While I studied political science in college, enamoured by the possibility of being able to join the foreign services, delayed graduation results didn't allow me to pursue this dream. Not willing to waste more time, I enrolled myself in a B.Ed course, which was then followed by a six-month teaching stint. I had met Amit by then, a third-generation entrepreneur, through some common acquaintances. Truth be told, I couldn't be happier to find him, the man who would be my husband. I was equally happy to be a part of his family and build a family of my own.

Coming back to my unpreparedness at Amit's passing, even during that last month in hospital, I did not think that this was the end of the twenty-two blissful years we had spent together. In fact, it was only about three hours before his death that it finally dawned on me that this resilient man, who had never let his ailment get the better of him, was unlikely to get better. Even that afternoon, when the doctors told me that they had changed the line of treatment, I was sure that he would respond to it. By 6 p.m., however, I started to realize that things weren't looking good and around 8.30 p.m. I understood that life was going to change forever. The end came at 11.29 p.m.

There was a lot to contend with. The gaping emotional hole that Amit's passing had torn into me was debilitating. Most importantly, I also had my children to take care of. My son was at an extremely impressionable age and my daughter had just about begun university in Scotland and had to be called back for her father's funeral. I recollect how, despite my distraught state and the fact that the house was teeming with well-meaning people, I had insisted that I be at the airport when she landed; my comforting presence was the least I could offer her at that time.

Surprisingly though, the one thing that was crystal clear to me, even in the days immediately after Amit's demise, was that I couldn't leave his business unattended, even though I knew virtually nothing about the construction chemical manufacturing industry. This despite the fact that we had never discussed the issue earlier, that we had never had wives or daughters joining the family business up until then and that I had no training or experience whatsoever that qualified me to do the job. As life would have it, I didn't even have the customary eleven days to mourn his death. On the tenth day, I had to meet with our lawyers as a branch of the family, which had earlier separated from the business and with whom we were locked in a legal battle with regard to the brand, had upped the cases. Amit had passed away on 25 February and on 10 March I remember walking into his office for the first time.

If you ask me what gave me the strength to take this decision, I don't really think I can say exactly what it was. Perhaps it was those twenty-two years that I had spent with the family business, purely as an onlooker, where I had imbibed the fact that my husband didn't just consider his work as a profit-making enterprise but also as a huge social responsibility. I recalled the many dinner table conversations where he was hugely mindful of the fact that one wrong decision on his part meant immense suffering for a worker's family back in a remote village.

To say that I could have sold out is an understatement. I recall the millions of conversations where people tried to counsel, coach and pressurize me to sell the company as I didn't have the requisite training or experience to run a construction chemicals manufacturing firm. Irrespective of the pressure, there was one thing I was certain of: I had to carry this company forward to the fourth generation. The brand CICO had seen a long journey from pre-Independent India, having been launched in the 1930s, and my husband was a third-generation entrepreneur. In fact, CICO's ad was on the *Statesman*'s front page on 15 August 1947 and there was just no way I could sell this legacy to an outsider.

The fact that 45 per cent of the company stake was held by a UK government fund didn't make the process any easier. They went to great lengths to explain how selling the company and holding on to the money would give me better returns than actually running the business. They were, however, conversing with a wall. All I did during that meeting with them was to keep repeating the one line on which my life depended: 'But I don't want to sell.' I guess they just gave up convincing me after a point in time. Today, of course, I am the 100 per cent owner of the company, having bought out those very investors. It was only much later when someone pointed out that statistically only 5 per cent of entrepreneurs are able to buy back their shares that the import of the act finally sunk in.

The early days, however, were a struggle as I contended with my complete lack of knowledge of the industry. To the credit of the CICO team, they went quite some distance to make me feel at home. In fact, I can never forget my first day at CICO when a senior team member, a gentleman who had been a part of the company's long journey, walked up to me to say, 'Don't worry, I am there to guide you'. Small acts of solidarity such as this in those trying times felt like they were god sent.

However, if there is one extremely moving incident that is stamped in my memory, it has to be the first Vishwakarma puja I performed in the company a few months after Amit's death. I was told that post the puja in the factory, the workers would come and apply tilak on my forehead and that I should keep some envelopes ready to be handed over as baksheesh. Nothing, however, could have prepared me for the actual turn of events. After the puja, not only did the workers apply a tilak on me, they touched my feet and, with folded hands, said '*Aap hamarey annadata hain* (You are our bread giver). Remember that there is food in 200 homes because of you.' I froze; there was no way I could stop my eyes from welling up. This was no longer about me or my children alone, I was accountable for over 200 families and that was a huge responsibility that I had to live up to. If there was even an iota of doubt in my mind about whether I had done the right thing by joining the business, this incident put all my doubts to rest.

The one thing that I was determined to do was to give the business my all and tackle all the challenges I faced headlong. And there were plenty of challenges; the greatest being my lack of technical knowledge. I remember speaking to a consultant back then and sharing my worry of not having the requisite expertise. I was able to draw strength from his words and I have tried following them ever since. He said that when a leader brings passion and commitment to the business, everything else falls in line. To this day, while I wish I had more technical knowledge to be able to take decisions across the table, I think my commitment to the business has made up for everything else. In fact, in my experience, when you are brave enough to admit your vulnerability to people, they open up and go to great lengths to help you.

I still recall an incident where I was meeting the vice president of a large organization in Bangalore for a possible business deal and he had some technical queries. I had no qualms in admitting up front that I did not know the answer to those technical questions. However, if he allowed me to connect him to my research and development head, I could ensure that all his queries were attended to. For the MD of a company, admitting lack of knowledge may not make for a pretty picture, but not only did he accede to my request, we later went on to do business together. Till now, I do not have any hassles in telling people that I do not know something, instead of striving to appear perfect. I do not think sharing our vulnerabilities is a sign of weakness at all; what is important is that we are honest in our dealings, and we accept our strengths and failings in equal measure.

If, on the one hand, I was making my way over a rocky road, my kids were undertaking an emotional journey of their own. My parents, who were too old and too grief stricken at my loss, came to live with me for a couple of years. I was relieved as it meant that my son didn't have to come home from school to an empty house. My daughter, by this time, was back at university to finish her course. It was much later that she told me how, having gone back after missing a part of the session, the university wanted her to enrol for grief counselling and repeat a year. She confessed how she fought her way through the ordeal as she explained to the officials that she had enough family support and hence did not need for any formal grief counselling and that repeating a year was a luxury she could ill afford. It was only after she won this battle did she let me get a whiff of her troubles; each of us clearly wanted to protect the other from further heartbreak.

If there is one other thing I recall from those early years, it is how I had turned into a social pariah overnight. For about a year of widowhood, I stopped receiving any invites to social gatherings that Amit and I were so much a part of. While this may seem inconsequential today, I remember how it bothered me those days to think that I was being punished for no fault of mine. Of course, now I would like to give them the benefit of the doubt as perhaps people don't really know how to deal with others going through a period of intense grief. Perhaps by not inviting me, they wanted to save me the awkwardness of coming to those gatherings alone and missing Amit even more.

Tragedy makes you stronger in more ways than one. What else can explain the fact that in the face of so much flux, I persevered and focused on the business, learning its ropes? In the early days, of course, people undermined my abilities, though I would like to think it was more on account of my lack of knowledge and not so much because of my gender. Having said that, there are some roadblocks that only women face, and these cannot be wished away. In my industry, which is totally male dominated, for example, a lot of business gets transacted over drinks and dinner; an old boy's club of sorts representing dominance and, of course, the exclusion of women. While women may have begun entering this club, it is still a long and arduous journey we face. But if there is something even more disconcerting for me than this sense of entitlement and inclusion that men seem to have, it is the total apathy when it comes to basic facilities for women. I still can't get a 2009 incident out of my mind, which occurred when I was travelling to Gujarat to look for a factory site. When I wanted to use a washroom, I was absolutely appalled to learn that there was no facility for women in that place. What they could offer me was a little cubicle whose door didn't shut fully. It was, at best, a tiny hole in the floor and there wasn't any water available there. This one time I remember having tears in my eyes. I felt really insulted, almost abused as a woman. These are the real challenges on the ground. I would go as far as to say that trials such as these bog me down much more than when I have had people threatening me over my business decisions, thinking that I would cow down as a woman. There have been other instances where just seeing a lady at the helm, employees have assumed that they will have to deal with someone really temperamental. However, none of this stereotyping has affected me as much as that day when I stood helpless, denied basic hygiene facilities.

Looking back at my journey, the one life lesson I have learnt is that mind wins over matter if you want to get somewhere. There are no roadblocks that cannot be crossed if you set your mind to it. I was fortunate to be invited for the Dell Women's Entrepreneur Network (DWEN) event held in Austin a couple of years back where I heard Brené Brown, a scholar and an author, give a lecture where she spoke of the importance of vulnerability in a forum titled 'Bold Beginnings, Brave Futures'. The fact is that you cannot be both brave and comfortable. Each of us has to make our own choices about whether we are content to stay in our comfort zones or whether we want to step out of them even if the process is excruciating.

It is a matter of great pride for me that in the process of stepping out of my comfort zone I could make a contribution to society. Today CICO's revenues stand at Rs 87 crore, up from the Rs 37 crore when I started out in 2008, fearful and inexperienced. We are now daring to dream big and hope to achieve our Mission 100—a goal of achieving the revenue of Rs 100 crore over the next year and a half. In fact, I recently came across a research report which names CICO as a 'key market participant' and the only Indian company among global players such as Dow Chemicals, RPM, WR Grace and other such behemoths. It is things like this that keep me charged. What is important though is that after five minutes of backslapping, you need to get back to work knowing that the world is looking at you and you cannot rest on your laurels.

Over the years, I have had many women ask me if they can also make the transition to being entrepreneurs from homemakers. I always say that as long as you have passion, commitment and good managerial skills nothing is impossible. As women running entire households, we are intrinsically good managers anyway. I feel the discipline with which I handled my home came extremely handy in the business world as well. When I took over CICO and called for a meeting at 10 a.m., people would casually saunter in late, whereas I work with the clock and get hysterical if things do not happen on time. Today, however, all employees have reminders on their calendars and if a meeting is called at 10 a.m., they ensure that they are there on time.

The other thing that women bring to the business table is the human aspect. After joining CICO, I put together a value document with some of its main tenets being integrity, passion, innovation and respect for all, as I felt we needed to do business with a human face, not just for profit margins. It was strange that while writing this document, I recalled writing a political science exam in college where I had forgotten a particular article number of the Constitution of India. It so happened that the person sitting in front of me lifted up her question paper and, without any effort, I could see the missing article number. While I jotted it down on my paper, when it was time to hand over the answer sheet, I couldn't live with my conscience telling me that the marks I would get for that answer would not be because of my capability or hard work. I scratched out the answer. Business is no different. All you need to do is follow the values that are intrinsic to you as a human being. The development of my team members rather than profit alone continues to be the guiding principle for me.

Today my days are full, what with managing work while also keeping my various interests alive. In keeping with my outdoorsy nature, I go out for long walks and play golf. I also love to take family holidays with my children, especially as both of them are currently living overseas and these holidays are the only time I get to spend with them. Running the Amit Gupta Foundation for organ donation, in the memory of my late husband, also gives me a lot of satisfaction.

The one thing that keeps me going is reading Swami Parthasarthy's Vedanta regularly. As he says living well is an art, a skill. I believe that irrespective of what happened yesterday, we need to keep moving ahead. The one thing I do not want when I am on my deathbed is to be filled with regrets. On days that I am down in the dumps, I also listen to Brahma Kumari Sister Shivani. Something that she says and what totally resonates with me is the fact that you have to look at life not as outwards in, but as inwards out. It is not all right to say that the other person upset you with his or her behaviour and, hence, you reacted in a certain manner. While his or her behaviour is his or her choice, getting upset is yours. I totally steer clear of negativity as it can sap your energy, leaving you with little strength to do anything productive.

My children, of course, continue to be my biggest strength. In fact, I believe that I am a mother first before any of the other roles that I play. It, therefore, gives me the biggest satisfaction to see that I have been able to fulfil my responsibility of raising children who contribute to society positively and stand up for the community. While my son keeps pushing me in all my endeavours, my daughter is my biggest cheerleader. Though my children are absolutely free to carve their own career paths, it is encouraging to know that my son is keen on coming back to India and taking over the business after another two to three years. Having brought the company so far, I am looking forward to stepping back from day-to-day operations and pursuing my other interests, although I will, of course, continue to be on the board to guide him with my experience. While running CICO for me was an accident, for my children it is going to be a choice. I am happy though to see them exert this choice and become the fourth generation to take over their family legacy!

Life Lessons

- ✓ When a leader brings passion and commitment to the business, everything else falls in place.
- ✓ There are no roadblocks too big if you put your mind to it.
- ✓ You cannot be both brave and comfortable.
- ✓ You cannot rest on your laurels. Take time to celebrate, but also get back to work as soon as you can.
- ✓ As long as you have passion, commitment and good managerial skills, nothing is impossible.
- ✓ While as women, particularly as mothers, it is our first priority to develop our children into responsible adults, who, in turn, can go out into the world and contribute, it is equally important that we do something more— for our communities, for our own selves.
- ✓ Irrespective of what happened yesterday, we need to keep moving ahead today. You have to look at life as inwards out and not as outwards in.
- ✓ Negativity can bog you down and sap you of your energies.

8

Jyothi Reddy

~

Founder, Key Software Solutions Inc., a software development and information technology consulting firm with a turnover of Rs 96 crore

Moment of Truth: Hearing her child cry 'Amma' just as she was about to take her life, followed by the realization that the onus of providing a better life for her children lay entirely on her shoulders.

From being married at the age of sixteen and toiling away as a daily labourer for a paltry wage of Rs 5 to keep her home fires burning to founding her own business empire, Jyothi Reddy's stellar rise seems nothing short of a fairy tale. She refused to get beaten down by her circumstances—whether it was living in an orphanage as a child or surviving a hand-to-mouth existence post marriage. She chose instead to build her own destiny when she walked out of the confining boundaries of her village and set out on her entrepreneurial journey. Having witnessed poverty up close, this Global Indian award winner (2012) is now a vocal champion for the cause of orphan girls—her mission being to ensure they have access to opportunities that would otherwise not come their way.

Destiny's Child

'Change your thoughts and you change your destiny.'
—Joseph Murphy, author

I am not an orphan and yet I spent over five years of my life in an orphanage in Warangal. My earliest childhood memory is of the seven of us—my parents, my four siblings and I—sleeping in a single file on a mat in our one-room home. My father was an ex-military man who gave up his career in the Army to become a farmer, but unfortunately could not make a success out of it. There was barely enough money to feed all of us. This extreme poverty forced my father to look for free accommodation for my sister and me. Eventually, he decided to put both his daughters in an orphanage where we would be offered food and basic education, while his sons continued to live with him. We landed up at Bala Sadan orphanage after being forced to lie to them that we were motherless. I was in class five, barely ten years old and my sister was even younger.

I remember crying myself to sleep every night, unable to share the truth with anyone out of fear of being turned out of the orphanage. In the five years that I spent there, I must have barely seen my mother three or four times.

It was a hard life to say the least; I used to walk barefoot to school every day and I remember being envious of children who had socks and shoes to wear. My biggest dream those days was to own a school bag. Things got so tough for my sister that she eventually ran away from the orphanage, back home, determined never to return. While I too longed to go home, my father had made it very clear that I was not welcome back, and so I had no choice but to continue at the orphanage. Even my holidays were spent there, helping the superintendent with the cleaning and other administrative stuff. I was good at my studies and passed the class ten exams with a first division. My dream was to become a doctor, but, of course, I was not exactly destiny's favourite child back then. My father told me bluntly that he did not have money to let me continue with my studies any further and had arranged for me to get married to a distant cousin—a small-time farmer, who was almost ten years my senior and lived in a village about forty kilometres away from where my parents stayed. I was very much against this marriage, but women in my community are not allowed to take any decisions for themselves. Besides, I knew that if I did not agree, it would be my mother who would end up bearing the brunt of my father's anger and I did not want her to get beaten up on my behalf. So I acquiesced; a dowry of Rs 10,000 was all that was required to absolve my father of any further responsibility towards me.

If I thought that life at the orphanage was tough, the next phase turned out to be even worse. From being a schoolgirl, I became a homemaker overnight, at the age of sixteen, when I moved in to live with my husband and his family. Not only did I need to work in my husband's fields, very often I had to work in other fields as well for a paltry sum of Rs 5 daily. By the time I was eighteen years old, I was mother to two daughters and my life had hit rock bottom. My day was divided between working in the farm and taking care of my home and my daughters. Despite working around the clock, there was never enough money to buy food or basic medicines for them, leave alone clothes or toys. Poverty often breeds extreme anger and it is sufficient to say that my family life was far from great.

One day, after a particularly bitter fight with my husband, I felt as if I could not go on any further. This was clearly not the life I had envisaged for myself and I decided to end it all by jumping into the village well after throwing my daughters in there first, in order to save them from the same plight. I had barely walked a couple of steps towards the well with my elder daughter, then aged only two and a half, when my one-and-a-half-year-old younger daughter, sensing something amiss, cried out 'Amma' in alarm. That one word broke something in me and I knew I could not bring myself to kill my children and myself. That night, I wept my heart out. But it also awoke in me a new-found resolve to seek a better life for my kids and myself. As a first step towards this, I reached out to my father thinking that anything would be better than staying in such abject poverty, but I was told that since I was married, my place wasn't with my parents. I realized then that I would have to seek out my own path, irrespective of whether I got any support or not. I owed my children a better life.

I started seeking job opportunities while continuing to work on the farm. I was fortunate enough to find that break I had been seeking so desperately; I enrolled as an adult education teacher under the Nehru Yuva Kendra scheme. I had to get other adults to join the night school and teach them the basics of reading and writing for the princely sum of Rs 120 a month. I was happy as I could finally buy food and medicines for my children. My next assignment, after over a year of working as an adult education teacher, was as a National Service Volunteer, responsible for touring villages to teach women and the youth how to stitch clothes in order to help them become earning members of their family. I jumped at the opportunity, especially since the new job came with a salary of Rs 190 a month, a big increase for me at that time. I wanted to send my daughters to an English-medium school, but of course I could not afford the fee. Even to get them admitted to a decent local school, I had to take a loan from a cousin.

While more opportunities meant I was earning more money, it also meant a lot of tension at home. One night, when I missed the evening bus back home after my duty and got very late, the family was livid and starting abusing me. Something snapped inside me that day, and I decided that I was not going to accept this as my fate. The very next day, I left the village along with my two daughters, a small iron suitcase in hand and a mere Rs 120 in my pocket, for Warangal, about 35 kms from the village Mailaram, where I lived. I was told that if I ever stepped outside the boundaries of my home and village, I would earn a bad reputation and it would be difficult for me to come back. But I was determined to make something of my life and remained unfazed.

I took a small room on a monthly rent of Rs 60. I did not waste a single moment of the day in a bid to build a better life for my daughters. Besides continuing with my job, I started stitching petticoats for Re 1 per piece. I, however, knew that if I needed to improve my lot, I had to find a way to upgrade my skills. Around this time, I learnt of a typing class nearby and decided to enrol there. I can still recall how I entered the class on the first day and all the other students, assuming that I had come to clean the room, starting vacating their seats. I didn't let the incident unduly affect me as I realized that you learn to get past these indignities in order to find your path in life.

One day, I saw an advertisement by Ambedkar Open University for a bachelor's degree. The one thing that worked in its favour was that the fee was Rs 320, which I could afford. Additionally, classes were held only on Sundays, which meant I could use the rest of the days to add to my income. My husband, who would come to visit us in the town off and on, severely opposed this decision. However, by then I had reached a point where I was past caring. Not only did I complete my graduation, I also went on to do my post-graduation from that university. After I graduated, I got posted as a special teacher in Ameenpeta village and later was promoted as a *mandal* girl child development officer.

It was around this time that fate smiled on me for the first time; I had a chance encounter with a cousin who had come down from the US on a vacation. One look at the way she carried herself and I knew this was the kind of life I wanted for my daughters. At that moment, I knew that the US could perhaps be my passport out of this cycle of poverty. On an impulse, I asked her if it was possible for a person like me to travel to the US and earn a living there. Her response is still etched in my memory. She gave me the assurance I so desperately needed when she told me that 'an aggressive person like you can easily succeed in the US'. I so desperately wanted to change my fortune that I went ahead and enrolled in computer software classes based on just this assurance. It took a lot of effort as I had to make the long commute every day from Warangal to Hyderabad to attend the classes. By then, I was obsessed with the idea of going to the US, as I wanted to live life on my terms. Very much against my family's wishes, I used up all the money I had saved so painstakingly and somehow got my passport and visa. It was most heart-wrenching when I had to leave my daughters behind in a hostel, with the belief that I would soon be able to offer them a better lifestyle.

Landing in the US with only $1000 in my pocket and two boxes filled with my belongings, I was excited and nervous at the same time. However, I had faith in myself—after all, if I could make it this far only through sheer hard work, then I knew I could do what it took to succeed in this new place as well. I managed to arrange PG accommodation with a Gujarati family for $350 a month and I took up whatever odd jobs came my way. From being a babysitter to a sales girl at a cassette shop, a gas station attendant to working in a motel, I did it all. I remember walking three miles every day back and forth to work.

That's when an acquaintance told me about a job opening as an IT recruiter at a monthly salary of $1000. I faced a lot of problems as I did not understand enough English. So strong, however, was my resolve that I started reading the Bible in a bid to learn the language. However, after working for some time, I was forced to resign since I didn't have a work visa. I went back to working for just $5 an hour doing odd jobs until the day I finally managed to receive my work visa. Getting the visa stamped in Mexico was really a eureka moment for me. I realized at that moment that I knew the ins and outs of the paperwork involved in getting a visa. Armed with this knowledge and my savings of $40,000, I set up operations in Phoenix in 2001. From having trouble filling up my passport form due to my poor English skills, I now help technology graduates from the best colleges in India secure a job in the land of their dreams. A feat, I believe, I have been able to achieve on account of my willpower alone. Having started out small, today the business has a turnover of $15 million.

Once I started earning a decent amount of money, I went back home and managed to arrange for my daughters to come to the US. Today, both my daughters are college graduates from US universities, work in the IT industry and are happily married. If nothing else, I am grateful to my husband for giving me the two biggest joys of my life—they are the reason I fought so long and so hard against my circumstances. Without their presence in my life, I might have perhaps accepted my fate and lived the life of a poverty-stricken homemaker. I am a strong believer in the fact that you control your own destiny. Of course, there is no permanence in life—today you might be living in a palace, tomorrow that same palace might be razed to the ground by an earthquake; but it's entirely up to you how determined you are and how much hard work you are willing to put in to change your circumstances.

As women particularly, we need to have the courage to pursue our dreams and not let anyone or anything stop us. To compromise or settle for less than what you think you deserve is really like short-changing yourself. I remember seeing an aeroplane in the sky whilst I was working as a farm labourer and I promised myself that I would be on that flight one day. I finally managed to come to the US aboard a Cathay Pacific flight with a ticket bought with my own hard-earned money. I was so obsessed with my dream that I never let the voices of doubt pierce my armour. Today, those same voices cannot sing enough praises of my success and achievements. I speak at plenty of women's forums and I firmly believe that it is very important for women to be self-reliant. To homemakers who want to turn entrepreneurs, I have three key messages—do not make undue compromises, remember that no condition is permanent and nothing is impossible.

I hope that my story energizes many other women to build a life for themselves. Just the other day, I was at a forum where a young girl, whose father is an auto driver, heard my story and came on to the dais to promise me that she will stand on her own feet before getting married. It is instances like this that make me feel that the troubles I went through in the early part of my life had a larger purpose. The one cause that is particularly close to my heart is the cause of orphaned children, especially young girls who are often forced into prostitution. I visited an orphan home in Hyderabad, where six of their girls had given birth to babies and were living in the same home with their kids. I am really concerned by the fact that the state government has released data on orphan boys who are in state remand homes, but the data for girls is conspicuous by its absence. If I can use my voice to do something for these girls, I will consider myself lucky.

Today, I feel humbled with all the awards that I have received; they have even included a chapter on my life in Kakatiya University's English lessons. I accept all of this with utmost humility and in the hope that it will inspire others who have given up on their dreams to once again find their inner strength to pursue them.

Life Lessons

✓ As women, we need to have the courage to pursue our dreams and not let anyone or anything stop us.

✓ It is very important for women to be self-reliant. Even if you do something small from home, don't give it up for tomorrow you might need it more than ever.

✓ To homemakers who want to turn entrepreneurs, I have three key messages: do not make undue compromises, no condition is permanent and that nothing is impossible.

9

Anuradha Pegu

~

Designer, founder of Naturally Anuradha, a brand specializing in traditional ethnic wear with a turnover of over Rs 40 lakh

Moment of Truth: An unfulfilled promise to her father to build a life for herself beyond the traditional role expected of women.

Belonging to a small tribe in a nondescript village in Assam, where women are expected to remain in the shadows of their husbands, Anuradha Pegu has lived much of her life debunking stereotypes to carve out her own success story. With patrons like Sonia Gandhi and Jaya Bachchan proudly wearing her signature saris, she stands tall as the designer responsible for bringing northeastern weaves into mainstream fashion in India and abroad. Not only has her collection been showcased in major fashion shows, she has also been awarded with the National Award (2010–11)—a fitting testament to her contribution to the industry.

Weaving a New World

'The mystery of human existence lies not in just staying alive, but in finding something to live for.'
—Fyodor Dostoyevsky, Russian novelist and philosopher

I was born in a village in Assam and am a part of the Mishing community, which loosely translates as the 'river people of Assam'. A large part of my childhood was spent watching and revering the mighty Brahmaputra, the river that serves as a lifeline for my community. My father was one of the relatively well-to-do farmers and a lot of my success today can be attributed to his progressive views, which helped shape my identity to a great extent. Not very educated himself, he had big dreams for his children and wanted all of us to be financially independent. With eight children and limited resources, he did his best to give us a good education. I can distinctly recall the palpable pride on my father's face as he went about telling people how his son went to Don Bosco school, despite his limited means.

The northeast is home to over 270 ethnic groups and communities, each with a distinct culture; barring a handful of tribes, nearly all the communities have their own individual weaving style. In fact, weaving is the exclusive preserve of Mishing women, who start their training in the craft even before they reach their teens. My mother was considered an expert weaver and I learnt the art at a very young age by simply watching her weave. It was incredibly fascinating to see the designs come to life beneath her fingers. My fate might have been similar to many other women in our community who weave their own articles for their dowry, get married and live a quiet domestic life—had it not been for my father who sent me to stay with my brother at Dibrugarh to continue my education after class eight. Encouraged by my father, I went on to complete my class twelve exams. While I was looking for something to do after that, I came across a year-long 'Training Demonstrator' course being conducted by the Sericulture Training Institute of the government of Assam. I went ahead and joined it. Generally, you get a government posting immediately after completing the course, but as luck would have it, the year that I passed out, there were no postings available. I was awfully sad about not being able to fulfil my father's dream, but with time on my hands, I decided to indulge my hobby and got three looms installed at my father's home. Friends and neighbours absolutely adored my work and I had my hands full.

As time went by, my parents wanted to see me settled and started to look for a suitable match for me. My wedding was soon arranged by family elders. It was 1995 and my would-be husband ran a transportation business. After my wedding, I moved to the city to live with him. My love for weaving, however, stayed with me and I decided to have my loom moved to my marital house. While my husband was supportive of my passion, I was in for a rude shock however. Unlike my village, where a loom was present in every home, here I faced stiff opposition from the neighbours who started to complain about the noise it created. I customized the loom using a tin box filled with mud to muffle the sound. I was determined to not let anything come between me and my passion for weaving.

Other than that, I took to my homemaker's role with elan. Soon, I was in the family way, expecting my elder daughter. As luck would have it, it was during this time that I received my posting letter from the sericulture department. While I had to decline the offer on account of my pregnancy, I remember being filled by a deep sense of wistfulness. Life, however, continued in its own trajectory and two years down the line, when I was expecting my second child, opportunity knocked once again. But I had to decline the offer again for the same reason a second time. This time my father was even sadder than I was, as this was the kind of service he had always envisioned for me and he was heartbroken to see the opportunity slip away from my fingers again.

While I continued to look after my home and family, there was always a lingering sense of loss, the sense of an unfulfilled promise. The feeling was especially heightened since many of my siblings could not make it big in their careers, despite my father investing in all our education.

Three years later, I finally had the opportunity to fulfil my dreams, by way of another letter from the Assam sericulture department. This time around, I went ahead and accepted it, even though it meant juggling my responsibilities as a parent of two young children with my professional life. If I thought I was finally being given the chance I was so desperately waiting for, I didn't know of the many other miracles that were in store ahead.

As I started working in the department, the one thing I did not forsake was my love for weaving. My hand-woven sarees became quite a rage and soon I was weaving sarees for people in my workplace as well. My flair for designing and weaving got noticed by the director of the sericulture department, and he assigned me to work with a professor from National Institute of Design, Gujarat, on a United Nations Development Programme–commissioned project. Working on the project was an amazing learning experience as it gave me an insight into contemporary concepts and methods of textile designing.

By then, the demand for my saris had grown so much that I started toying with the idea of taking it up commercially. My husband's transportation business was on a downside at that time and so I managed to convince him to rent a house where I could set up looms, employ artisans from my village to start selling these saris commercially.

That is how 'Naturally Anuradha', a brand that has grown since, came into being. The superior craftsmanship resulted in the products becoming popular by sheer word of mouth. The next big growth spurt came when I started participating in exhibitions. The early days were far from easy though. My first exhibition, I recall, was in Chennai. Participating in these exhibitions meant that I had to travel—a fact that didn't go down very well with my husband. Travelling also meant spending money. I would be extremely frugal as I undertook the long journeys by train. Added to this was the fact that in some of the early exhibitions, I was often given a very small space with no visibility on account of the fact that my brand wasn't well known.

In one such exhibition, I remember not even being provided with a table and I had to use the trunk in which I had carried the saris to display my collection. However, good work speaks for itself, and my organic collection, embodying the essence of nature, sold out within an hour, while others with much better display and visibility still had a lot of inventory remaining. There have been other challenges as well; travelling for exhibitions required leaving the children behind for several days at a stretch, which is never an easy task for a woman. There were times when my husband got fed up with my busy schedule and even asked me to give it all up.

I still recount those times with horror—for instance, when I was travelling and one of my kids had fallen ill. In such times, I was so overwhelmed with guilt that I wanted to catch the first train back home. To add to my despair, there were more than enough relatives branding me 'selfish' for leaving an unwell child at home. My in-laws have been supportive, but in my community, a woman's place is considered to be her home and everything else is considered secondary. There have been times that I have felt absolutely alone and have spent many a night weeping. Despite everything, I struggled to continue working because giving up weaving was simply not an option for me—it is such an inextricable part of who I am.

From participating in exhibitions to being part of the Lakmé India Fashion Week (LIFW), it has been a long road, made possible only by tireless work and everyday sacrifices. I had never dreamt of participating in the LIFW, it was almost as if the opportunity presented itself when they decided to introduce the 'Made in Assam' initiative in partnership with the Northeast Fashion and Design Council. The idea was to showcase the distinctive textiles and weaves of the northeast, with a view to increase their appeal and wearability. The discussions with LIFW had been going on for more than two months, but, in the end, I got only about a month to create the entire collection. It was a crazy time—I had to work night and day to procure the raw material, design and prepare the final collection. However, the overwhelming response to my show more than made up for the effort that my team and I had put into the collection. LIFW opened new doors for me, and brought national and international recognition to my brand.

Receiving the National Award was also a classic case of luck meeting talent. The director of the Weavers Service Centre chanced upon my work and was so impressed with it that he told me that I deserved a National Award. I took it as a compliment and did not give it another thought. Some days later, he came to my home, inquiring if I had applied for the National Award. I had not so much as heard of these awards before and had absolutely no clue of how to go about applying for it. While I kept dismissing his suggestion, he was extremely persistent. So strong was his faith in my talent that he finally filled up the form himself and presented it to me for my signature. All he asked me to do was '*accha sa ek* piece *banao* (craft a great piece)', as it was mandatory to submit a sample of one's work with the application. I didn't even prepare a special sari to submit for the National Award, instead I submitted one that was already in the works. Imagine my utter shock and delight then on winning the National Award! It was a humbling experience to say the least, and it vindicated all the struggle and hardship I had undergone over the years to make my craft visible to the world. Starting my days at 4 a.m. to ensure I could get through all my work, staying away from my children just to get my work out in front of a wider audience, collaborating with many artisans to put together designs that could do justice to the rich heritage of my land—all my efforts were now justified as I received the National Award from the President of India. There have been other awards since, but the National Award will always remain very special to me.

If I have one regret today, it is that my father isn't with me to witness my success. I could not even be by his bedside during his last hours. We were in Shimla on a vacation when he passed away. There isn't a single day when I do not miss my dad, and I constantly think of how proud he would have been of my success. My mother too passed away soon after, leaving a huge void in my life. I know that they are blessing me from above and that is how I am crossing so many milestones today.

My advice to all women looking to become entrepreneurs is to remain strong even when you face stiff opposition from all quarters. I feel there is a lot of talent in Assamese women; with each tribe having its own unique weaving patterns, you can imagine the kind of versatility that exists in our rich culture.

Entrepreneurship, I believe, is all about committing to your passion. There is no place for any ifs and buts here. There are many occasions when women may just give up because they feel that they can't do justice to their families, particularly their children. While this is partly true, it is also a reality that our children do not need us to be physically around them all the time. Both my daughters are doing well in their studies, even though I was not always available to teach them myself in their formative years. My elder daughter is now in her second year of textile designing at college and my younger one is giving her class twelve board exams this year. Even now, there are times when my husband gets a little irritated seeing me checking my mails and responding to messages while the children are at home. He wishes that I spend more time with them and tend to my work only in the hours that they are away. I, however, know that my children are independent enough to take care of themselves. Besides, my work demands that I respond to customer queries without too much delay. Seeing my work being appreciated by people all over the world and the look of sheer pride on my daughters' faces when I cross another milestone really makes it all worthwhile. More than anything else, what also gives me the impetus to carry on is the fact that I have been able to provide livelihood to so many artisans whose lives have been changed forever now.

My dream for tomorrow is to be able to provide financial independence to many more women of my community and elsewhere in the northeast by providing them with training in business and running skill development programmes. I also want to incorporate a society that provides opportunities for women to start their businesses by incubating them. This will not only empower the women of my community but will also help in reviving the traditional weaves of my land.

Life Lessons

✓ Women entrepreneurs need to remain strong even if they face opposition from the people closest to them.
✓ Entrepreneurship is about committing to your passion.
✓ There are several occasions when women tend to give up because they feel that their children need them. However, children do not need us to be physically around them all the time.
✓ I dream to provide financial independence to women in the northeast and elsewhere by training them in business and running skill development programmes.

10

Rakhee Vaswani

~

Professional chef, TV show host, author; founder, Palate Culinary Academy, with a turnover of over Rs 1 crore

Moment of Truth: A life-altering conversation with her children encouraging her to reclaim her love for cooking.

> Rakhee Vaswani's journey from a stay-at-home mother to being hailed as one of the leading chefs in India is one of sheer dedication to her craft. After being pushed into rekindling her passion for food by her children, she gave it her all, leaving no stone unturned in her effort to make her new innings a successful one. Rakhee learned quickly that just passion is not enough to sustain a new venture, so she chose to invest time,

money and effort into learning from the best chefs in the world early on, a move that has paid her rich dividends. She is hailed as the 'desi Nigella Lawson' today and is frequently seen hobnobbing with celebrity chefs from all over the world. Her culinary studio offers over 150 classes and boasts of an impressive line-up of students.

Adding Flavour to Life

> 'A recipe has no soul. You, as the cook, must bring soul to
> the recipe.'
> —Thomas Keller, American chef and restaurateur

For as far back as I remember, food has played an important role in my life. I'm a Sindhi and I must have been about eleven years old when I first whipped up a Sindhi curry for my family and I have fond memories of just about everyone absolutely relishing it. There were many more occasions for me to discover the joys of the kitchen, especially since I lived in a large building where all our neighbours were like family to us. I was often to be found happily lolling around in the kitchen of one of the neighbours in the building watching them cook. Every household has a distinctive style of cooking, and I started revelling in and imbibing the different flavours, spices and recipes from as young an age as eleven. The only disconnect I faced with food was that I was a picky eater and since my brother suffered from poor vision, my parents took it upon themselves to ensure that I ate a healthy diet. I still recall how my father would bribe me with a Rs 50 note to finish my carrot juice.

I attended my first informal cooking class, learning Chinese cuisine, at the age of thirteen or fourteen, from a neighbour. A quarter of a century later, the memory is still fresh in my mind, almost as if it happened only yesterday. It was a eureka moment for me, for I had discovered something that gave my life purpose and meaning. I could not get over my excitement, to the extent that each day for one whole week my entire family was subjected to the same menu—sweet corn soup and hakka noodles, prepared by the budding chef Rakhee. A large part of my childhood was spent staring at magazines filled with photographs of delectable dishes that I so wanted to recreate. However, despite feeling so strongly about food, there was never an opportunity to receive any formal training in the art of cooking during my formative years.

Growing up in a typical Sindhi household, your expectations are fairly set—graduate from college, get married and raise a family. I had prepared myself mentally for this journey, but it so happened that I met and fell in love with my future husband when I was just in class ten. One of the things that brought us together, and still continues to bind us, is our common love of food. Even though he is not a chef, my husband is a food connoisseur in his own right; he understands food and can talk about it for hours and is one of the best food critics I have met.

We got married immediately after my graduation with our parents' consent and I set out on an exciting journey. I was twenty-two-years-old then and I remember that even though I was thrilled to be married, I had a strong urge to develop a career that involved cooking. With a supportive partner in tow, I started offering cooking lessons from my home. However, family life beckoned and soon I had my hands full managing a child. The effort to juggle my multiple roles took a toll on the time I could spend with my baby, and it led to the unhappy realization that I needed to put my dream on hold. I soon gave up teaching in order to devote time to the biggest priority in my life: my family. Another child followed soon after and life for me pretty much revolved around my home and hearth. It wasn't as if I had given up my love for cooking altogether, as I would keep experimenting with different dishes and would use every opportunity to cook for friends and family. My vacations abroad in these years almost always had me checking out a local cooking academy and its state-of-the-art equipment and courses. Somewhere, deep down within me, was this wistful longing to reunite with my first love—cooking.

After spending more than eight years as a contented homemaker and mother, it was my children who took it upon themselves to rekindle my love affair with food. Come to think of it, it nearly happened overnight—as if it was a decision just waiting to be made. One evening, while discussing the day's happenings with my husband, I happened to tell him about how the kids had told me that they were old enough to take care of themselves, and that since I loved cooking, I should do something about it. My husband immediately took the discussion up several notches as he started to discuss the logistics of how I could make a new beginning. My family often quips now that 'we only encouraged you to start your cooking classes simply to get you out of our hair', but beneath all this banter I know that they realized how much I missed sharing my love and knowledge of cooking with others.

While all this sounds pretty easy, I was setting out on this journey at the age of thirty-eight. You can well imagine my fears of stepping out of my comfort zone, if I may call it that. My husband went on to rent a garage space for me to build a culinary studio on a three-year lease. My fears were so potent that I went back to the landlord to renegotiate a two-year lease. I did not want my husband to spend an extra year of rent on the place if things did not work out. Even though my husband kept assuring me that I need not worry about the rent, in my mind I was very clear that if I had to get back to work, I had to run a self-sustaining operation.

While I devoted my heart and soul to setting up the studio and started running my classes, I had a nagging feeling that even though I was passionate about cooking, I wasn't up to speed with the latest trends. I felt that my passion had to be matched with the latest skills for me to deliver something truly world class. Clearly, I felt that I could not restrict myself to the classes I was presently conducting. Keeping this in mind, I enrolled myself in a host of short-term courses—I joined the Professional Masters Education (PME) course in sugar craft from the International Institute of Culinary Arts, Dubai, and I also decided to enrol for a six-week Le Cordon Bleu certificate at Gordon Ramsay's Tante Marie in London. In hindsight, the course helped me tremendously as it not only gave me a functional edge, it, more importantly, gave me the confidence to start all over again. I remember getting back from the course feeling rejuvenated and invigorated. The course made the pain of leaving my family behind for almost two months well worth the effort.

My journey now formally began from the garage studio, with a set of ten one-day workshops, where I taught almost all the trending cuisines and dishes—sushi, Thai, Asian, Continental, Mughlai, etc. being only some of them. During this period, I had a steep learning curve. While I had updated my culinary skills, the fact is that I had never run a business before. Many tools of business that are so important in today's world were absolutely alien to me then. I began in the old-fashioned way of personally calling people up and informing them of my classes. People were intrigued by my concept of one-day workshops, since most classes in those days were of longer duration; and so I had a good start. However, I soon realized that in order to scale up operations, I needed to learn the concepts of social media marketing and the like. In my technologically challenged state, it took me nearly a year to set up a good website, but I was determined to do everything I could to make my venture a success. Similarly, little by little, I learnt more about the concept of food photography. My early attempts to have the perfect dish photographed met with little success for no matter what I would do, the coriander would sink into the curry faster than the photographer could say cheese! It was quite a shocking discovery for me to learn that those pictures of delectable dishes that I gazed at for hours in my childhood were not real images, but were dressed-up pictures.

Armed with my new-found knowledge and with my hard work, the classes started gaining popularity, enabling me to increase their frequency from once a week to about four classes a week. We continued growing and expanding in this manner for three whole years, until, eventually, a shortage of space began to limit my capacity to take in more students in my garage studio. This is how Palate Culinary Studio was born in January 2013 in a much larger space. While I started by taking all the classes myself, as the number of students grew, I slowly expanded my team to include many talented professional chefs from the industry, who were passionate about teaching their craft. What makes the classes interesting is that I do not just teach a recipe but also go the extra mile to make the dish look attractive. Today, I offer over 150

cooking and baking classes, and I feel blessed that my life
has touched the lives of so many students—from budding
five-year-old bakers to seasoned eighty-five-year-olds.
Driven by the studio's popularity, I have also had a whole
lot of Bollywood A-listers as my students. Recently, I had
Arjun Kapoor in my studio as a part of his preparation for
his role in the movie *Ki & Ka*. To be honest, I was quite
impressed by his dedication; even though the role did not
demand him to do any actual cooking, he made sure that
he learnt how to chop, grind and cook a variety of dishes
from scratch. All this, while we had eight news channels
covering us live in the studio. As a teacher, my proudest
moments, however, are when I see budding chefs who
have literally grown up cooking at my studio whip up
dishes with ease.

Interestingly, my food adventures have helped me
embark on many new journeys, my TV show being one
of them. It all started when I was given an offer to join
MasterChef as a participant. I remember declining the
offer at the time as I had just started Palate Culinary
Studio then, my third baby of sorts, and all my energies
were focused on making it a success. My first TV stint,
therefore, came when I did a short programme for the
newly launched Living Foodz channel. I remember that
in one of the baking special episodes, I taught audiences
how to make masala bread. That evening, my Twitter and
Instagram feeds were filled with pictures of the viewers' own

attempts at making the masala bread. Those pictures felt like a kind of a tangible vindication for all the efforts that I had put in to work towards my passion. I try to make all my shows as close to real time as possible so that people can cook along with me during the show and enjoy the process. My show 'Rewind with Rakhee' for Living Foodz channel was an amazing experience. The show launched around my birthday in 2015, and it was a great feeling to see billboards and posters of my cookery show all over Mumbai on my birthday. The show gave me an opportunity to explore my dramatic side, and each episode saw me don a new avatar. The first season was based on exploring cooking trends from the 1900s and for each episode I assumed the character of an iconic woman from that era. One of the best episodes was when I played Mother India on screen, replete with all the nuances of the character. The show was an instant hit and soon I was being offered other TV shows, like Super Foodz in which I would travel to meet chefs from all across the country and the world, and explore their kitchens.

I have had the opportunity to travel and meet food gods like Chef Raymond Blanc and Eric Lanlard, and I learnt a lot more about the art of cooking from them. One of my favourite experiences was meeting with Chef Ajit Ramon from Jaivilas Oberoi, who put up a royal sample menu based on the diverse culture of India for the show.

Today, I am also an author with my book, *Picky Eaters*, a throwback to my own days of picky eating. My aim with this book is to make it possible for every parent to cook healthy food, which looks fun and exciting too, at home. Malaika Arora, my long-time student and now a dear friend, released the book and I have been overwhelmed to see the support I have received.

A teacher once told me that the more you share, the more you learn, and I have found this adage come true in so many ways. Even after teaching 150-plus courses in my studio, I still find something new to learn every day. More often than not, the learning comes from my students, whose curiosity leads them to explore and discover new recipes. Today, my dream is to start my own culinary college that offers world-class programmes. While I could go and acquire a certification abroad, I feel there is no reason why India shouldn't offer such a high-quality platform wherein budding chefs can get certified right here. I am on my way to realizing this dream as, apart from offering different kinds of cooking and baking classes, Palate Culinary Studio has become the only institute in India authorized by the Confederation of Tourism and Hospitality (a professional body that confers qualifications in culinary arts) to offer a UK-certified culinary award course. I will continue to build the studio to offer many more courses that can help budding chefs gain a foothold in the magical world of food. At the same time, however, I hope to add to my own repertoire of learning. After all, it is going to take many more lessons and sharing on my part to be able to lay even a tiny claim to becoming a great teacher when it comes to the art and science of cooking.

The one lesson that I have learnt in my entrepreneurial journey is that it is never too late to give wings to your dreams. If you are enthusiastic about something, there is a lot you can do to realize this passion. It doesn't matter whether you are fifty or even sixty years old—you just need to begin somewhere. Having said that, there should be no compromise on learning. Really, learning does not come with an expiry date. A certificate against your name always adds weight to your profile and, most importantly, it fills you with confidence. What can also help your learning curve is to have a mentor who can help you navigate the tricky road to entrepreneurship.

I think as women, we have a natural instinct for business. Not only are we focused on what we want to achieve, our ability to empathize with the emotional needs of others around us gives us a big advantage. Our only disadvantage may be that we are conditioned to second-guess our own abilities. However, this isn't something that one cannot overcome with conscious effort. As for me, I have been blessed with a very supportive husband who has been my biggest cheerleader. There isn't a single news clipping about me that he hasn't painstakingly circulated amongst family and friends with immense pride. I also derive a whole lot of strength from the look of pride on my children's faces on every such occasion. My daughter is

twenty and my son is seventeen now, and I sure hope that
I have equipped them with a strong sense of hope as they
get ready to take on their individual careers.

Life Lessons

✓ The more you share, the more you learn.
✓ It is never too late to give wings to your dreams. As
   long as you have a passion for something, there are
   many ways in which you can realize your dream.
✓ Learning does not come with an expiry date.
✓ Since the road to entrepreneurship is filled with pitfalls,
   having a mentor will come in handy.
✓ As women, we have a natural instinct for business. We
   can focus on what we want to achieve and our ability
   to empathize with others lends us a huge advantage.

11

Sundeep Bhandal

~

CEO, Anjaneyap Global, a management consulting and technology services company with a turnover of Rs 320 crore

Moment of truth: Her inability to buy a toy for her son brought on the resolve that she needed to earn enough money to never face such a situation again.

Entering the United States, the so-called land of opportunity, as a young bride, Sundeep Bhandal, ironically, had to brave a mindset that deemed a woman's stature to be below that of her husband's and that her place in society is confined to the home and the hearth. Not willing to allow her identity be constricted within these narrow perceptions, she continued to forge ahead bravely, armed with nothing more than self-belief. Undeterred by the many challenges she faced along the way—be it the lack of finances or family support—she successfully set up her staffing firm, Anjaneyap Global, that clocks a revenue of approximately $50 million today, proving that success knows no gender.

Against All Odds

'Your present circumstances don't determine where you can go; they merely determine where you start.'
—Nido Qubein, motivational speaker

I grew up in a small town in India, where the only aim of educating girls is to ensure that they get married into a 'good family'. Having said that, my family was quite progressive. My grandparents, in particular, were highly liberal in their thinking. After migrating to Rajasthan from the other side of the border during Partition, they had to start their life again from scratch and, therefore, laid a lot of emphasis on working hard. I grew up watching my grandparents lead by example and, hence, I have family values and hard work engrained into my DNA. My grandmother would constantly urge all her grandchildren, including the girls—a rarity back then—to focus on their studies. In fact, I recall how if I ever took to sewing or embroidery, she would admonish me to finish my studies first. My father too encouraged me to explore new avenues; being a woman was never a valid reason to not undertake any project. Unlike other families, I was allowed to venture out of home without a male escort and pursue my hobbies and interests. In fact, I remember being the first girl in my town to drive an open jeep. It used to be quite a sight to see the expressions on people's faces as they spotted me behind the wheel, with my hair flying all over my face. Comments from friends, relatives and neighbours notwithstanding, my parents never thought of clipping my wings. As a child, I remember wanting to be a cop and fighting injustice, but as the daughter of a lawyer, I ended up pursuing law. It was during my final year of studies that life took a sudden turn in the form of a phone call from my grandfather.

Visiting family in Canada and the US, my grandfather happened to meet my future husband at a social gathering. Impressed by the young man's sense of responsibility towards his family, he called home straightaway from the US, resolute in his decision about getting me married to him. In hindsight, I wish I had not given in to his decision so easily; however, back then, my grandfather's word was law for me. Barely out of my teens and yet to figure out my life's purpose, I had no reason to oppose his decision. Besides life had been hunky-dory for me till then and my young mind couldn't fathom the possibility of it being anything else. Once the ball was set rolling, things happened really fast. I got to meet my to-be husband for the first time only on the day of the wedding! Once the marriage ceremonies finished, my husband left for the US, while I stayed back to complete my studies. I eventually left for the US in the new millennium. I remember stepping out of the protective confines of my father's home with stars in my eyes. Little did I know what fate had in store for me. Brought up in a liberal household, I could hardly have anticipated a home with a highly traditional mindset, especially with regard to women. While women in the household were expected to be subservient, when it came to daughters-in-law, the rules were even more stringent. Not used to such barriers, I often found myself speaking out of turn, which was not very well received by my in-laws. Soon, I learnt to keep my thoughts to myself, simply to preserve peace at home. A decade later, I still recall how my husband would often tell me that I was not like other girls. The remark was clearly not meant as a compliment; it was more about my tendency to not be cowed down and my propensity to speak my mind. Living in a joint family also did not make things easy for me. All I remember of the first few years of my marriage is this terrible feeling of homesickness that engulfed me. I yearned for the freedom that I had taken so much for granted at my parents' house.

Money was tight because my husband was the only earning member in the family. I had a strong desire to get out of the home and do something with my life, which would also ease the financial burden on my husband.

However, I was scared of voicing my thoughts for fear of disturbing the equilibrium at home. Eventually, with some coaxing, I managed to get my husband's consent to enrol in an accountancy course, which could help me secure a small-time accounting job at a local office. However, destiny intervened, this time in the form of the birth of my son. I had to take a break from the classes to focus on taking care of my newborn. Motherhood brought about profound changes in me; for the first time in my life, I was fully responsible for the well-being of someone besides myself and I gave in to the feeling completely. I wanted to shower my son with all the love and happiness in the world, and it was this feeling that really brought about a moment of awakening in me. I still distinctly remember being at Target, the supermarket, along with my son, looking for bargains, when I happened to wander into the toys section. There was this little soft toy that my son happened to lay his hands on. He didn't have much by way of toys on account of our limited financial muscle and, on an impulse, I decided to purchase this one for him. I remember putting it in the cart, but no sooner had I started wheeling it towards the billing counter that doubts began to creep in.

The toy was not too expensive, but it was still more than what we could afford at that time and I began to think of how my household budget might be impacted on account of this impulse buy. As I stood there, weighing the pros and cons of my decision, I was suddenly consumed with a sense of self-pity. The fact that I had to think so much before buying a small toy for my son filled me with shame. I made a vow to myself that day that I would never allow myself to be in this situation ever again in life—that I would earn enough to ensure that I did not have to think twice before buying something for my son. As a homemaker, that too in an unknown, far-off land, I had no idea whatsoever how I would be able to fulfil this promise.

With this resolve, I rejoined the accounting course and decided to take up a job in a small firm. As luck would have it, I finally ended up at a staffing firm as a payroll executive and it was here that I gained first-hand knowledge of the workings of the IT industry. It was while working here that I chanced upon the opportunity of opening a Subway franchise and was rather taken by the idea of being my own boss. The family was far from supportive and I had to use up all my savings and seek help from friends to take the big step of buying my own franchise. As I could not afford to employ people at that stage, I found myself taking on myriad roles—owner, sweeper, cleaner and server. From getting up at the crack of dawn and purchasing supplies to preparing subs for customers, tendering cash and mopping the floor and cleaning up, I have done it all while taking care of my duties at home.

Maintaining this kind of a schedule day in and day out was tough to say the least. My hard work, however, paid off, as within a year I found myself with enough spare cash to purchase another franchise. Now, my time was divided between the two franchises, while taking care of my son and ensuring my home and family did not suffer in my absence. Along the way, however, I realized that the food business was really not for me as I missed the white-collar, structured and professional atmosphere of the IT industry.

As luck would have it, around this time, I happened to meet someone who was looking for a partner in his staffing firm and I jumped at the opportunity. Being a partner, however, required an investment far beyond my limited resources. When I shared the opportunity with my husband's family, they were quick to ridicule it, and asked me to forget it and concentrate on my home instead. I then took the bold step of approaching my father for the money required for investing in the partnership. My parents have always been the bedrock of my life; within days, the money was transferred, no questions asked. Matters remained tense on the home front though, with questions being asked about my ability to run a business and what my contribution to the household was likely to be. I, however, remained steadfast through all the uproar and decided to follow the path I had chosen.

Life became a blurry haze of days going by in quick succession. For a while, I continued to be involved in the Subway business, while also investing in the staffing business. My first shift of the day would last approximately eleven hours, from 6 a.m. to 5 p.m., and I would alternate between the two franchises. I would then reach Anjaneyap, my staffing firm, to start the second shift of the day only to reach home somewhere around midnight. My day, however, didn't end there, as I still had to take care of my household chores. There were days when I would break down completely from the sheer pressure of it all. My only regret from those days of working day and night is that I missed out on spending time with my son. I, however, took solace in the fact that he was growing up in the joint family set-up.

As for Anjaneyap, the initial years proved to be extremely tough. We started off as a single-client company and continued to remain like that for a very long time. If there was one thing that helped me survive those odds, it was my faith in my own abilities; and extreme financial prudence. We ran a very tight operation in those initial years, which meant that I had to take up a lot of work upon myself. From running the payroll to filling legal paperwork, client relationship building and even taking care of office maintenance, I did everything. I spent a lot of time networking as well in those early days in order to gain leads. Even after we finally managed to break the one-client jinx, we continued to operate with a very small team for a long time in order to save costs and increase our profitability. We were sure that we did not want to make the mistake that many start-ups make—of trying to expand too fast too soon. Those years of skimping and saving is what helped us build a war chest that has fuelled the rapid expansion that Anjaneyap has seen in the last couple of years. It was a dream come true to see Anjaneyap being listed among the 500 fastest-growing companies in the US in 2012. That it is a zero-debt company and all our expansion has been totally self-funded makes the achievement even more special.

One thing that helped me in my initial years was the extensive networking I did. It is on account of this that we were finally able to come out of the one-client curse and there has been no looking back since then. However, being a young woman entrepreneur has been far from easy, even in the developed US economy. I have encountered enough and more instances of when clients would not take me seriously, directing all their questions instead to my male partner. Compared to my partner, I think I have had to put in twice the effort to earn the same level of trust. What I have learnt in good measure though is that it is important to build effective relationships with even the most difficult clients. Lucky to have been blessed with good relationship-building and convincing skills, I have always ensured that I go the extra mile and become the go-to person in case of any client issues. In fact, I would recommend that women entrepreneurs work on their networking skills. In a bid to juggle our many roles, we do not pay sufficient attention to this aspect of business and unwittingly pay the price for it.

The one piece of advice, however, that I particularly want to give budding women entrepreneurs is never to give up. The journey may be long and tortuous, but you need to work with a single-minded focus towards your goal.

You are also bound to encounter many naysayers along the way, who will go out of their way to tell you that a woman's place is only at home with her family. Burdened with all of this, there will be times when you will start to doubt your own capabilities, but as long as you live and breathe your dream every single day, you are bound to succeed. While all of this may sound like a cliché, I have seen this come alive in my own life journey.

As support from my husband and in-laws dwindled and relations reached breaking point, I decided to take an irrevocable break from my fractured past. While the dreams with which I came to the US didn't quite work out, there is a lot I have today for which I am very grateful. My son is my biggest source of pride. When he calls me a 'super mom' and eggs me on to do so much more, I am filled with an unflinching zeal. The only regret I have is that amidst my personal and professional struggles, I could not spend enough time with him in his growing years, something that I hope to correct now—even if it means cutting down on my work commitments. The one value that I hope I have instilled in him in abundant measure is that of respecting women.

My parents live with me now and it is their support that has kept me going in the darkest of times. Today, they are incredibly proud of my achievements. I know that they often talk of my success to their friends back home. If my story can inspire other young girls to make their own destiny, I would think my own journey has been worthwhile.

Life Lessons

- ✓ I would recommend that women entrepreneurs work on their networking skills. Many women let go of this in their bid to juggle their roles, and they have to pay the price for it in their professional journeys.
- ✓ Never give up. The journey may be arduous, but you need to work with a single-minded focus towards achieving your goal.
- ✓ You are bound to encounter many naysayers, but it is important you do not listen to them and pursue your goal.
- ✓ As long as you live and breathe your dream every single day, you are bound to succeed.
- ✓ I am what I am today because of my struggles.

12

Pabiben Rabari

~

Founder, pabiben.com, a women artisans enterprise that has a turnover of over Rs 20 lakh

Moment of Truth: Gifting a self-designed 'Pabi bag' to a foreigner attending her wedding and landing international orders based on that one gesture.

When Pabiben Rabari, an unschooled but extremely enterprising woman from a nomadic tribe in Kutch, decided to present the traditional embroidery of her tribe to the world, she not only gave herself a new identity but also gave the craft a new lease of life. While her designer handbags, christened 'Pabi bags', have garnered both national and international recognition, with her eponymous brand, she has turned women from the hitherto little-known Rabari community of Kutch, Gujarat, into proud breadwinners for their families. From being honoured with the Janaki Devi Bajaj Puraskar (2017) to having her bags featured in Bollywood and Hollywood movies, this barely educated woman from a little-known tribal community in the hinterlands of Gujarat is an inspiration for many.

Threads of Change

'The secret of change is to focus all of your energy, not on fighting the old, but on building the new.'
—Socrates, Greek philosopher

I belong to Kutch, a land known for its rich artistic traditions. A part of the nomadic Dhebaria Rabari community, I had a traditional childhood. Like with any other family in our tribe, my father was a herd grazer. As a little girl, I used to see him leave with his herd early in the morning before I left for school. I was barely five years old and my younger sister was just three, when tragedy struck. My father died suddenly while tending to the herd, leaving us destitute. My mother was pregnant at the time with my third sister. With the onus of running the household falling on her overnight, she started to work as a labourer in order to provide for us.

Given the changed conditions of our household, I had to drop out of school when I had just about completed class four. Till today, I regret not getting the opportunity to complete my education; but then again, life has rewarded me in other ways. I remember doing small chores at the time, including filling water for people's homes from the village well for Re 1 to help keep the home fires burning.

Early on, I also learnt the art of embroidery. My tribe, the Dhebaria Rabari, is known for the most elaborate and intricate embroidery, characterized by chain stitches and mirror work. A lot of the embroidery was done to create dowry pieces to accompany a new bride.

My mother was an expert at embroidery, and since I was at home, I had ample time and many opportunities to learn from her. It was around this time that an NGO came to my village in a bid to expand their artisan base. As a young girl, I was looking for ways to help my mother run the household and I was quick to jump at this opportunity. Not only did I join the group, I was soon appointed the local teacher to lead the programme in the village. I remember getting a salary of Rs 300 a month, a huge increase in my earnings in those days.

I would have also ended up creating my own dowry pieces had it not been for a diktat passed by the elders of the community banning embroidery for personal use. They had a good reason to do so, as the tradition of girls embroidering their dowry articles was leading to what they saw as a 'disturbing trend' of women continuing to remain at their parents' homes till as late as thirty-five years of age to ensure they had embroidered enough pieces. Seeing no other way of stopping this trend, embroidery was banned for personal use altogether. While the ban was welcomed by many—as it relieved girls from spending their youth toiling over the embroidery—it also sounded the death knell for the beautiful handcraft.

While we had no choice but to comply, we started to think of alternate methods of continuing with the craft, and this is how 'Hari Jari', the application of ribbons and trims using a machine, came about. We started lace work and machine work as an alternative to heavy embroidery for our own consumption. It was fascinating to see how what would take us months to embroider by hand could be done so fast and efficiently by machines. Soon, I was busy conceptualizing designs that could be created using sewing machines for not only garments, but bags, cushion covers, kits and quilts.

With the hand-embroidery ban in place, my marriage was fixed at the young age of nineteen. As was the norm, the match was arranged by my family elders; my to-be husband worked at a *kirana* shop. If I look back, it is fascinating to see how my journey as a homemaker, that began subsequently, was inextricably linked with my entrepreneurial journey. A group of foreigners, charmed by Indian traditions, happened to attend my wedding. They saw the bags crafted by me and were extremely delighted by the craftsmanship. Seeing their fascination, I decided to gift them a bag. Little did I know at the time that this innocuous gesture would lay the foundation for my entrepreneurial journey. This little bag that they carried back with them later went on to become an international hit and was christened the 'Pabi bag'.

In the meantime, as I settled into my new role as a homemaker, I also started working for an NGO that saw great potential in the bag and started to market it domestically. They would pay me around Rs 60 for every piece and I happily started to earn money while managing my household.

After working with them for several years and witnessing the popularity of my bags did I begin to consider the possibility of branching out on my own, in order to give more voice to the craft of my community and to be able to earn better. I must admit that I was very apprehensive of starting out on my own. While I was adept at creating the products, I was not at all confident about the selling aspect as I had little experience of dealing with buyers. While my husband kept encouraging me to branch out, I somehow could not garner the confidence to do so. The thought remained in my head for almost five years before I finally took the first step towards my entrepreneurial journey.

I remember how it took me a while to decide the name of my enterprise. I have always felt that the artisans who actually create the beautiful products do not get enough recognition for their craft. It was with this thought that my eponymous brand, Pabiben, came into existence. In the digital world, since no business can exist without an online presence, it got rechristened as pabiben.com. As for its tagline, 'Rediscover the Artisan', it was born out of seeing women artisans forsaking their traditional craft. In fact, ever since the massive earthquake that rocked Kutch, life here had undergone dramatic changes. In a bid to rebuild their lives, many women artisans had joined industries as daily wage labourers. I was really pained to see this and thought it was time to reconnect these artisans with their craft.

Once I set out on my journey, things started falling in place and I was grateful to see many people coming forward to help me. I remember getting my first large order worth Rs 70,000 from a showroom in Ahmedabad, followed by an international order of over 1000 pieces. In fact, in the very first year of operations, my venture had a turnover of Rs 20 lakh. It wasn't so much the money but the fact that I was doing something meaningful for the craft of my region that gave me a huge high.

My husband, who so far used to help me out in my work as and when he could, now gave up his job at his kirana shop where he earned a salary of Rs 15,000 a month and joined me full time. His support has been of huge help to me. I am very fortunate to have been blessed with a partner who has always encouraged me to seek my own path, even at the cost of facing ridicule from members of the tribe. Women in my community are generally not allowed to work outside the home, leave alone go outside the village selling items. When I first started to go for exhibitions all over India, people used to make fun of my husband, telling him that if he gave me so much freedom, he could be certain that his wife would run away some day. But my husband refused to pay any heed to these baseless comments and remained steadfast in his support. Now that I am successful, the same people who used to taunt my husband earlier keep telling him how proud they are of my achievements and are now ready to extend support to my endeavour as it is benefiting our community immensely. The one lesson I have learnt is that beyond a certain point, one needs to follow one's own trajectory without bothering too much about what people say. I have also been lucky to get a lot of support from my relatives—for instance, my aunt and cousin came to help me out at an exhibition in Surajkund this year, after which we set up a stall at the Kala Ghoda Festival in Mumbai.

I have also been lucky to have support at home when it came to raising my children. With all three of her daughters married, I was worried about my mother living alone and had brought her to live with me; although, the community did point fingers at me for breaking yet another custom. I was, however, unfazed as my mother's well-being was far more important to me than some age-old custom that forbids her from living with her married daughter. I must admit that in the beginning there were times when my own mother used to spend nights worrying about what I was doing travelling all over the country alone. However, I assured her that I would never do anything to break her trust. Today, she is my biggest cheerleader and is the greatest support system I could ask for.

While I started selling Pabi bags commercially about two years back, we have grown from being a single-woman enterprise to a group of fifty women who work together to make the brand a success. My wish is to take the number to 500 women. It is extremely gratifying for me to see women of my community no longer need to work in factories or fields as labourers. The worst part about working as a labourer, apart from the backbreaking work, is the fact that in the lean season there are many months when you have to go without work. If you happen to be living on daily earnings, like we used to when my mother had to work as a labourer, then a day without work could easily end up a day without food. Pabiben.com has helped these women get out of factories and work from the comfort of their homes. Also, my work is perennial, which means there is no lean season for which they have to start saving in advance. Pabiben.com has given them both financial independence as well as an opportunity to showcase their creativity to the world, while allowing them to preserve their cultural identity. Today, these artisans can effortlessly balance their home and work. We are firm believers in Gandhian principles, and all of us share the wealth we create through pabiben.com.

If I had any doubts about my venture being a success when I started out, today, when I receive many awards from industry bodies, it fills me with renewed determination to continue on my path. When I won the Janaki Devi Bajaj Puraskar for outstanding contribution to rural entrepreneurship in 2017, more than me, it was the other women of my community who were really proud of my achievements. Another special day was when I had the opportunity to meet Prime Minister Narendra Modi on the occasion of Women's Day. It was a memorable moment when I could gift him an iPad sleeve made by the women who work for pabiben.com

Today, our creations have made their way all around the world, including the fashion hubs of Italy, the UK, Spain, Switzerland, France, Germany, USA, Austria, Costa Rica, Australia and, of course, the national fashion hub, Mumbai. Having our bags used in popular teleseries and mainstream Bollywood movies like *Luck By Chance*, and also in the Hollywood movie *The Other End of the Line*, left us ecstatic. It gives the women of pabiben.com a tremendous sense of fulfilment when they see how far we have come from our humble beginnings. To be honest, even in my wildest dreams I had never thought I would come this far. It gives me joy beyond words when I see my son attending an English-medium school, something I could never have dreamt of without my enterprise.

The one thing that has stood me in good stead along my journey is that I never thought of giving up, no matter how hard the circumstances were. Maybe that is the reason for my success. My advice to other women who want to become entrepreneurs is to never accept defeat. Every one of us experiences struggles and obstacles; as long as you remain steadfast in your purpose, you are bound to find success. Also, I feel that support from home is necessary for women to make a success of their careers. My husband has been a pillar of strength in my life; in a community where women are not supposed to step outside the home, he stood by me as I chased my dream. They say behind every successful man is a woman, but in my case it is clearly my husband who is deserving of this credit.

Today, many women reach out to me saying that they want to be a part of my artisan group. While it makes me feel good, it also adds to my sense of responsibility as I need to ensure that together we grow from strength to strength.

Life Lessons

✓ Beyond a point one needs to follow one's own life trajectory without caring too much about what people say.

✓ I never thought of giving up, no matter how hard the circumstances were.

✓ To every woman who wants to become an entrepreneur, never accept defeat.

✓ Every one of us experiences obstacles along the way, but as long as you remain steadfast you are bound to succeed.

✓ Support from home is essential for women to find success in their careers.

Dare to Be Conversations

If you have made a life-changing journey yourself or you know someone who has or if you simply want to read many more inspiring accounts, please join the community at www.facebook.com/Daretobeconversations.

It is by sharing our collective experiences that we can drown out naysayers and, most importantly, drown out the persistent negative voice in our own heads.

Acknowledgements

The first thank you for this book has to go out to Gurveen Chadha, our editor, who, after our first book *Dare to Be*, suggested that we chronicle the stories of homemakers turned entrepreneurs. Thank you for leading us down not just a writing project but an extremely inspirational journey. Thanks are also due to Jyotsna Raman, our copy editor, and the entire team at Penguin Random House for subsequently bringing the book to life.

A heartfelt thank you to Anu Aga for so graciously agreeing to write the foreword. It is not just the fact that you have scaled great heights professionally but also your sheer humility that has awed me. I am sure many women will go on to write their own scripts, inspired by your journey.

I had an absolute fan girl moment as I interviewed each of the wonderful women whose life is chronicled in this book. After every interview, my spirit has soared on witnessing the strength of human will in the face of almost insurmountable odds. I strongly believe that there is some cosmic reason that my path has led me to so many inspiring women. Thank you for giving me the privilege of telling your stories. Many of you have turned from subjects of my book to friends for life and that is really special to me.

Thanks are also due to Kanishka Gupta, our agent; your unstinting support ever since we began our publishing journey has been very reassuring.

Writing could have been an extremely lonely process, but it was made far from solitary as I could brainstorm ideas with Puja Singhal, my co-author and childhood friend. Thank you for being a part of this journey.

My family is my biggest support system; thanking them just for this book, therefore, seems really inadequate. Nonetheless, for now, let me thank you for bearing the brunt of the many bouts of my midlife crisis, as I sat down to write. No wait, didn't I hear someone say (I think it was Anshu Mor, the stand-up comedian) that forty isn't a midlife crisis, it's just a standalone crisis? Well, whatever it is, a warm thank you to my husband, Sachin Sachdeva, for standing by me like a rock. Thank you, Vijay and Usha Paul, for being the best parents ever (Dad, I know you are watching me from up there). Thank you my darling daughter, Suhaani, and my ever-supportive in-laws. Thanks are due to my sister Dipti and her angel Ahaan, and to my sister Soma and her family. A warm thank you also goes out to my entire extended family, especially to my mamu and masis who have been my go-to people.

Without you, neither this book nor anything else in my life would have been possible.

— **Rinku Paul**

Thank you, Gurveen, both for your unstinting support during our first book as well as for suggesting the topic for our next. It is your motivation that has made it possible for us to meet the twelve highly talented and courageous women, whose stories are proof that one person can be the agent of change for an entire community. Thank you also to the Penguin Random House team, especially Jyotsna, for helping us share our writing with the world.

My sincere and heartfelt thanks to Anu Aga for continuing to bless our journey as writers in so many ways. I hope that you continue to shine your gracious light on us. My next thank you goes out to the brave and inspiring women featured in the book, for allowing us the privilege of sharing their stories with the world. Their courage and graciousness will continue to inspire long after the book is done and dusted.

A big thanks to you, Kanishka, for the generous support right from the start of our journey as authors.

Thank you, Rinku, for making this journey with me; your presence makes every part of the writing process memorable.

A big thanks also to my husband and children for putting up with all the ups and downs that accompany the process of writing. Thanks are also due to my parents, brothers and sister, who always remind me to keep striving and growing as a person.

—**Puja Singhal**

A Note on the Authors

Rinku Paul

A corporate career spanning over sixteen years with the news channel Aaj Tak, a part of the India Today Group, made up the first part of Rinku's career. Till she decided to pursue her dream—impacting people's lives!

She is now an internationally certified life coach, corporate trainer and neurolinguistic programming practitioner. In co-founding a writing studio, The Muse, she has also given her first love, writing, a professional outlet.

This is her second book. Her first, *Dare to Be: 14 Fearless Women Who Gave Wings to Their Dreams*, which she co-authored with Puja Singhal, was released to acclaim.

Rinku lives in New Delhi, with her husband and daughter.

Puja Singhal

With more than a decade spent in corporate life, strategizing how best to marry business and people as an HR specialist, Puja decided to take a break to focus on her family and other love, writing. Having co-founded a writing studio, The Muse, and published her first book, *Dare to Be*, along with Rinku Paul, she is now back to juggling corporate responsibilities along with family duties and, of course, writing.

This book is proof of the fact that it is possible to make time for the things we value in life.

Puja holds an honours degree in political science and an MBA in human resource management.